CLASSIC CARS

Marks and Spencer p.l.c.
PO Box 3339
Chester CH99 9QS

shop online
www.marksandspencer.com

ISBN 978-1-84805-416-5

Printed in China

Designed, produced and packaged by Stonecastle Graphics Ltd

Text by Andrew Noakes
Designed by Paul Turner and Sue Pressley
Edited by Andrew Charman

All photographs © LAT Photographic Digital Archive

Classic Cars

A CELEBRATION OF THE WORLD'S GREATEST AUTOMOBILES

Andrew Noakes

MARKS &
SPENCER

Contents

Introduction

Old cars have soul and character that very few modern machines can match. Modern cars are very safe, very reliable, extremely fuel efficient. They are often faster, invariably emit fewer pollutants and need infrequent servicing. Yet few of them offer the involvement and excitement of a classic, and none of them have the years of history that makes an old car special.

There are almost as many definitions of classic as there are classic car enthusiasts. The Classic Car Club of America has a very rigid definition, limited to 'fine or unusual' cars built between 1925 and 1948. As far as they are concerned, an Auburn Speedster is a classic but a Model T Ford isn't. Most enthusiasts take a more pragmatic and wide-ranging view, however, admitting to the ranks of classics all sorts of vehicles from the early days of motoring right up to modern machinery. Many of them are featured in the pages which follow.

Inevitably plenty of them are the rapid and sensational sports cars of each era – cars like Jaguar's XK120 and E-type, Ferrari's Daytona and 246GT, Lamborghini's Miura and Countach, and from America the Chevrolet Corvette and a whole host of V8-engined 'muscle cars' from the '60s. There are more affordable sports cars too, from the golden age of the British roadster – kicked off by cars like the MG T-series in the 1940s and perpetuated by Triumph's TRs, Austin-Healey's four cylinder and six-cylinder machines, MG's MGB and Triumph's Spitfire. Above them

Above: By some of the more strict definitions, the magnificent 'gullwing' Mercedes-Benz 300 SL does not qualify as a classic – but most enthusiasts would agree the term fits very well.

Below: The Auburn 851 Speedster is a classic in the eyes of the Classic Car Club of America, which recognises only the best cars from 1925 to 1948.

in the pecking order lie more sophisticated machinery from the likes of Lotus (with the Elite and Elan) and Porsche (with the 356 and 911). Meanwhile, Italy contributes the characterful sporting cars of Fiat, Alfa Romeo and Lancia.

But classic cars aren't all sports cars, or even the sports saloons which became popular from the 1960s onwards thanks to cars like the Mini Cooper. The classic ranks also include elegant coupes and cabriolets like the Mercedes Benz 300SE of the 1960s, and plush prestige saloons like Lincoln's 1961 Continental or the Rolls-Royce Silver Shadow – and many more.

More humble cars make the grade too, particularly those that have mobilised the millions thanks to clever design. Henry Ford's Model T has pride of place in these pages, and so too does Ferdinand Porsche's Volkswagen and Alec Issigonis' Mini, classics all of them.

Whether you are motivated by the thinly disguised racing cars on the road that have grabbed plaudits and headlines down the years, or the luxury saloons that offer the highest quality of engineering and design, or the everyday machines which wrought sweeping changes to our society and our quality of life, you'll find a classic car to excite you. And you'll probably find it in the pages that follow.

Above: Long-running popularity, engineering integrity and a remarkable competition career make Porsche's 911 a genuine classic.

Below: Speed and style at their peak: to many the Jaguar E-type is the ultimate classic car.

7

Mercedes 35hp-60hp

It was Emil Jellinek, a businessman living in the south of France at the start of the 20th century, who gave the name 'Mercedes' to the products of the German Daimler car company. The first Mercedes cars were the 28hp Daimler Phoenix models he entered in a hillclimb competition in Nice in 1900. The next Mercedes models were perhaps the most significant cars of their era.

Jellinek asked Daimler to produce a faster, lighter and better-handling machine which would be more competitive in sporting events. The response from Daimler's chief engineer, Wilhelm Maybach, was a car which set a pattern for performance cars which still has echoes today.

Maybach built a new 35hp engine with, for the first time, an aluminium crankcase to reduce weight. Conventionally intake valves had been 'automatic', sucked open by vacuum in the cylinders, but Maybach arranged positive operation by a camshaft to improve valve timing. With twin carburettors – one for each pair of cylinders – the 35hp engine offered sparkling performance together with unmatched smoothness. The chassis was equally innovative: for the first time, the side members were stamped from sheet steel to save weight.

The first 35hp was test-driven at the end of November 1900, and delivered to Jellinek that December. Early in 1901 it proved its worth at the Nice speed trials, and 'Mercedes' quickly became a household name. That autumn work began on an even quicker car, the 40hp 'Simplex', and by 1903 Mercedes had introduced the 60hp, good for a then-astonishing 60mph (96.6km/h).

Above: Wilhelm Maybach's Mercedes 60, a development of the 35hp car of 1900, set the basic layout which most performance cars would follow for decades to come.

Below: Innovations on the Mercedes included an alloy-block engine with positive exhaust valve operation, and a chassis made from pressed steel members.

Rolls-Royce Silver Ghost

The car which earned Rolls-Royce the soubriquet 'the best car in the world' was the 40/50hp – more commonly known as the Silver Ghost. For nearly two decades, the Silver Ghost was for many people the ultimate in motoring luxury. Launched at London's Olympia motor show in November 1906, the Silver Ghost was lavishly engineered, neatly detailed and exquisitely manufactured. It provided an almost unmatched blend of comfort, smoothness and performance.

The key to the Silver Ghost's ability was its engine, an in-line six-cylinder unit with the cylinders cast as two blocks of three. Unusually for the time the crankshaft had a full complement of seven bearings, further aiding smoothness and reliability. The bore and stroke were both 4.5in (114mm) resulting in a capacity of 7036cc and an output of 48bhp, with vast reserves of torque available at very low engine speeds. In 1907 that flexibility was demonstrated by Rolls-Royce managing director Claude Johnson driving from Bexhill to Glasgow using only third and fourth gears, in the silver 40/50hp which was the first to be called 'Silver Ghost'. The same car proved its quality time and again in long-distance reliability runs.

More than 6000 40/50hp models were built before Rolls-Royce moved on to other models in 1925. The original Silver Ghost, Johnson's 40/50hp, was sold by Rolls-Royce in 1908 but bought back 40 years later and today it is still owned by the company. It is unlikely ever to be sold again, but must be one of the most valuable cars in the world.

Above left: The imposing face of the 40/50hp Rolls-Royce, with the famous 'Spirit of Ecstacy' mascot atop the radiator grille.

Above: Exquisite workmanship and endless attention to detail were hallmarks of Rolls-Royce – this is the model that earned the title 'best car in the world'.

Below: Rolls-Royce built more than 6000 of the 40/50 model – better known as the Silver Ghost – between 1906 and 1925.

Ford Model T

Henry Ford built his first car in 1896 and went into production with the two-cylinder Model A in 1903. Four- and six-cylinder cars followed over the next few years, but it was the Model T launched in 1908 that really put the Ford Motor Company on the map.

Ford designed every aspect of the 'Tin Lizzie' for cheap and easy mass production, ease of use and ease of repair. In its basic layout it was very much a conventional machine, with a simple ladder chassis and separate body and an in-line four cylinder engine mounted at the front with its gearbox behind, driving the rear wheels through a propshaft and live rear axle. It was the detailing which made it clever.

The engine was a simple 2.9-litre unit with a cast iron block and cylinder head, side valves and a three-bearing crankshaft with crude splash lubrication. Maximum power was just 20bhp, but the engine developed plenty of low-speed torque. The engine was controlled not by an accelerator pedal but by throttle and ignition timing levers mounted on the steering wheel.

The gearbox was unconventional, and made the Model T much easier to drive than many rivals. Instead of a normal manual gearbox and pedal-operated clutch, Ford employed an epicyclic geartrain which offered two forward speeds, plus reverse and neutral. High and low gears were selected using the left-hand pedal, while the middle pedal selected reverse. The right-hand pedal operated a transmission brake.

Above: Ford knew most motorists drove on farm tracks or open country, so he fitted the Model T with transverse leaf springs to give excellent ground clearance.

Below: Model Ts were available with numerous different styles of bodywork, from chic two-seaters to taxicabs and trucks. This four-seater dates from 1915.

Ford realised that few American motorists had good roads to drive on: most had to contend with unmetalled farm tracks or open prairie. The Model T's suspension was designed with those conditions in mind. Both axles were mounted on transverse leaf springs, inverted so the centre of the spring was mounted on the chassis and the ends picked up on the axle. Though this resulted in a rather tip-toe appearance it gave the Model T excellent ground clearance to cope with the worst roads.

Ford sold 10,000 Model Ts in 1909, the first year of sales. As production quickened and the build process was further streamlined and mechanised, costs came down and Ford cut the price again and again – the tourer which had cost $850 in 1909 was just $360 by 1916, and in the same period Ford doubled his workers' wages and shortened their working day.

Production peaked at over 2 million in 1923, but by then the Model T was showing its age. More than 15 million Model T Fords were built in a production run which continued for 20 years, finally coming to an end in 1927. It made mass-production a reality, mobilised America, and expanded Ford's reach overseas. Crude though some of its engineering might be, the Model T is unquestionably one of the greatest cars of its era.

Above: Model Ts were fitted with a novel transmission operated by pedals – the throttle was a lever on the steering wheel.

Ford Model T	
Engine 2878cc in-line four	
Bore x stroke 95 x 101.5mm	
Valvegear Sidevalve	
Fuel system Holley carburettor	
Power 20bhp at 1800rpm	
Suspension Front: beam axle and transverse leaf spring; rear: live axle and transverse leaf spring	
Wheels Wooden-spoke	
Brakes Mechanical brakes on rear wheels only	
Top speed 42mph (67.6km/h)	

Bentley 3-litre/4.5-litre/ Speed Six/8-litre

The magnificent machines created by W.O. Bentley are among the most recognisable of all vintage cars. Massive, powerful and fast, they are among the ultimate machines of their era.

The 3-litre arrived in 1921. It was based on a stout conventional ladder chassis frame with huge side members, on which sat an unstressed body fronted by a characteristic rounded radiator. Under the bonnet was a four-cylinder fixed-head engine with a single overhead camshaft which was shaft-driven from the front of the crankshaft and operated 16 valves.

The 3-litre developed an impressive 80bhp, while the 4½-litre which followed gave 105bhp. Even more was on tap from the famous 'blower' 4½ and six-cylinder, 6½ litre Speed Six from 1929.

Ettore Bugatti is said to have described Bentleys as 'the world's fastest lorries'. W.O. Bentley built his cars to be strong, powerful and fast, and their record in competition shows that the strategy was a success: Bentley's cars beat the French in their own Le Mans 24-hour race four times in succession, from 1927 to 1930. But Bentley's sporting success was not matched in the marketplace: the Depression arrived just as the firm went into the super-luxury arena with its 8-litre model. Bentley went into receivership in 1930 and was taken over by Rolls-Royce.

Above: Bentley's first car was the four-cylinder 3-litre, unveiled in 1921. The 16-valve engine developed 80bhp.

Below: The 8-litre Bentley was built to take on Rolls-Royce, but arrived as the Depression started.

Bugatti Type 41 'Royale'

Despite the 'Royale' soubriquet, Ettore Bugatti's magnificently decadent Type 41s never found a customer among the European royalty for which they were originally designed. Instead just six of these enormous, 12.8-litre machines were built, three of them remaining inside the Bugatti family and the other three being sold to private owners.

The limited production run was certainly not a reflection on the quality of the car. Like all Bugattis it was immaculately well built, and blended style with clever engineering. Brake drums were cast integrally with the massive 24-inch alloy wheels, for instance, and the vast engine had three valves for each of its eight cylinders, all driven by a single overhead camshaft.

The Type 41's problem was its huge cost – more than twice the price of a Rolls-Royce – and the nose-dive in the world economy at the end of the 1920s. It was launched at just the wrong time.

Though the Royale was ultimately a commercial failure, its engine formed the heart of a high-performance railcar designed by Bugatti in 1931 and used on French railways in the 1930s. More than 100 railcar units were built, helping Bugatti to weather the economic downturn.

The super-rare Royale is, inevitably, one of the most valuable cars in the world. One example sold at auction in 1987 for $8.7million, by some margin the highest auction price ever recorded for a car.

Above: Vast and magnificent, the Royale is one of Bugatti's best-known cars – yet in commercial terms it was a failure. Everything about the Royale is built on a massive scale, from the 24-inch alloy wheels to the 12.8-litre engine.

1930 Bugatti Type 41 'Royale'	
Engine	12,763cc in-line eight
Bore x stroke	125 x 130mm
Valvegear	Single overhead camshaft
Fuel system	Single carburettor
Power	300bhp at 2000rpm
Suspension	Front: beam axle with semi-elliptic leaf springs; rear: live axle with quarter-elliptic springs
Wheels	24in alloy wheels
Brakes	Drum brakes all round
Top speed	125mph (201km/h)

Bugatti Type 35

Italian engineer Ettore Bugatti started building cars under his own name in 1909, but it was the Type 35 of 1924 which really put Bugatti on the map. This vehicle is the archetypal Bugatti: light, fast and built like a Swiss watch, advanced in some areas but frustratingly old-fashioned in others. The characteristic eight-spoke alloy wheels often fitted to Type 35s were one novelty, in an era when wire-spoke wheels were the norm. The 2.0-litre straight-eight engine was also innovative, with three valves per cylinder and five ball-race main bearings allowing it to reach 6000rpm and develop 90bhp. It also produced a very distinctive sound, likened at the time to 'tearing calico'.

Despite Bugatti's opposition to superchargers, a Roots-type blower was added for the 128bhp Type 35C. There was also a cheaper and less powerful Type 35A with plain bearings. Later the engine was stroked to 2.3 litres for the unsupercharged (and very rare) 35T and the supercharged 35B. The same chassis was also made available with 1.5-litre engines in the Type 37 and Type 39.

Bugatti's Type 35 was an extraordinarily successful racing car, winning hundreds of events including five consecutive Targas Florio in Sicily and the inaugural Monaco Grand Prix in 1929. It must also rank as one of the prettiest cars of the pre-war era. It's a combination which makes the Type 35 one of the most sought-after – and most valuable – of collectors' cars.

Above and below: Bugatti's Type 35 was a phenomenally successful racing car in the 1920s and 1930s. The eight-spoke alloy wheels are a distinctive – and innovative – Bugatti characteristic.

Alfa Romeo 6C

ittorio Jano's arrival at Alfa Romeo marked a revolution for the Milanese firm. Jano's first job was to lay out a new supercharged Grand Prix car, the P2. It was lighter and more streamlined than previous Alfas, and was powered by a new 2.0-litre straight-eight engine with twin overhead camshafts acting on inclined valves which fed hemispherical combustion chambers. The P2 was instantly competitive.

Its engine formed the basis of a six-cylinder, single-cam motor for a new generation of road cars, known as the 6C series, in 1925. With no supercharger and only a single carburettor the first 6C 1500 was relatively underpowered, but it was just the start of a range of cars which would become renowned for their speed and style. By 1928 a quicker twin-cam 1500 Sport was available, and that was followed by a high-compression Super Sport.

Even more performance was to follow, with the introduction of a larger 1750 engine, at first in single-cam form but later in twin-cam and high-compression guises. The latter, known as the 1750 Gran Sport, delivered 85bhp and a top speed in excess of 90mph (144.8km/h).

An eight-cylinder 8C series followed, but all were expensive cars which few could afford in the Great Depression. Eventually Alfa Romeo had to rely on government money to keep it afloat, and soon Italy was embroiled in war…

Above: Sparse interiors were the order of the day, particularly on sporting machinery such as the Alfa Romeo.

Below: Vittorio Jano developed the single-cam, six-cylinder 6C road car engine from the twin-cam straight eight race engine in the P2. The 6C series began in 1924 with the 1500, and continued after the war with cars such as this 6C 2500.

Duesenberg J/SJ

Brothers Fred and August Duesenberg built successful racing cars before branching out into luxury road cars with the Duesenberg Eight in 1921. But in 1926 the company came under the control of E.L. Cord, and as if the Eight had not been extravagant enough, Cord introduced a completely new Duesenberg which was bigger, heavier and even faster.

Introduced in 1928, the Model J was powered by a 6.9-litre straight-eight engine with twin overhead camshafts and four valves per cylinder. Despite its size and weight the Model J was comfortably a 100mph (161km/h) car, and customers looking for the last word in performance were catered for in 1932 with the introduction of an even more rapid supercharged SJ model. The Duesenbergs were favourites of America's rich and famous, including Clark Gable, Gary Cooper and Howard Hughes.

Though the J and SJ survived the Great Depression and continued to be built in small numbers during the early 1930s, the Auburn-Cord-Duesenberg combine as a whole struggled to make money. The collapse of the company in 1937 ended Duesenberg production, when fewer than five hundred of these amazing machines had been built. Today the size, the engineering and the glamour of these cars, together with their rarity, means that they are among the most sought-after and valuable American classics of all.

Above and below: Sweeping lines of the Duesenberg J hint at its impressive performance – though big and heavy, this was a 100mph (161km/h) car. This one was built in 1935, just two years before the failure of the Auburn-Cord-Duesenberg combine.

Mercedes-Benz SSK

F ew cars could catch an S-type Mercedes in the 1920s. Developed by Daimler's chief engineer Ferdinand Porsche, the supercharged six-cylinder 'white elephants' gave Mercedes numerous competition victories and paved the way for Germany's domination of Grand Prix racing between the wars.

The S – for 'Sport' – models were developed from existing Mercedes, with modifications to improve performance and handling. The S-types were lower than their predecessors, with larger engines mounted further back in the chassis. The supercharger was engaged only at full throttle, delivering 180bhp from 6.8 litres. It was with an S-type Mercedes that emerging maestro Rudolf Caracciola won the first ever Nürburgring race in 1927.

The S was replaced by the 7.0-litre, 250bhp SS ('Super Sport'), from which the SSK was developed. The K stood for 'kurz', German for short, indicating that the SSK had a shorter wheelbase for crisper handling. As well as being an effective racing machine the SSK was the road-going supercar of its day, and the longer-wheelbase S-types were favourites for comfortable and extravagant touring bodies.

The ultimate derivative of the S-type was the lightweight SSKL, its chassis peppered with drillings to reduce weight to the bare minimum – about 2976lb (1350kg), some 276lb (125kg) lighter than the standard SSK. With 300bhp from its 7.1-litre straight-six engine, the SSKL could achieve an extraordinary top speed of 157mph (253km/h). Caracciola took it to victory in the Mille Miglia in 1931, the first time the race had been won by a non-Italian car and driver.

Racing regulations changed in 1934, introducing a 1653lb (750kg) maximum weight which outlawed leviathans like the SSK and instead ushered in a whole new era of racing.

1929 Mercedes-Benz SSK	
Engine 7065cc in-line six	
Bore x stroke 100 x 150mm	
Valvegear Single overhead camshafts	
Fuel system Two Mercedes-Benz carburettors, part-time Roots supercharger	
Power 250bhp at 3300rpm	
Suspension Front: beam axle with semi-elliptic leaf springs; rear: live axle with semi-elliptic springs	
Wheels 20in wire wheels	
Brakes Drum brakes all round	
Top speed 117mph (188km/h)	

Below: Characteristic external exhaust pipes are a feature of the short-wheelbase SSK. A lightweight SSKL version driven by Rudolf Caracciola became the first non-Italian winner of the famous Mille Miglia race in 1931.

MG Midget/Magnette

C ecil Kimber ran Morris Garages, the Oxford sales and service operation which William Morris had established alongside the Morris Motors manufacturing firm from which the huge Nuffield Organisation had sprung. Under Kimber, Morris Garages began building sporting specials based on Morris cars. Ultimately they became a separate line under the name MG.

The car which really defined MG in the minds of sporting drivers everywhere arrived in 1928. It was based on the Morris Minor, Nuffield's answer to the Austin Seven. Unlike the crude Seven, the Morris Minor had a competent ladder-type chassis and an excellent overhead-cam engine of 847cc. MG's open two-seater version, the M-type Midget, began a series of compact roadsters which would be hugely successful for MG.

Above left: The M-type, based on the tiny Morris Minor, began a long line of successful compact sports cars for MG. Many cars were faster than the MGs, but few were more fun to drive.

Above: Cecil Kimber was responsible for the styling of early MGs, giving them attractive well-proportioned shapes which appealed to sporting motorists of the day.

Left and above: The K3 Magnette was one of MG's racing machines of the 1930s. MG was hugely successful at the banked Brooklands track, in the Ulster TT and even in sporting trials.

Chrysler Airflow

Some classics were very successful, but not all of them. The Chrysler Airflow, for all the technical innovation and ultra-modern styling which made it so advanced, was among the most heroic of failures.

The Airflow, launched in 1934, was one of the earliest examples of 'unitary' construction. There was no separate chassis, box-section load-bearing members instead being integrated into the pressed-steel body. Cost and weight can be reduced, and passenger space improved, using this type of construction. The Airflow's body was given very modern full-width styling with a smoothly curved, streamlined shape. A long-wheelbase Royal Airflow was also available.

In other respects the Airflow was conventionally engineered for its time. Three engines were available, a straight-six and straight-eights of 4.9 and 5.3 litres, driving through a live rear axle. Leaf springs were used all round, and hydraulic drum brakes were fitted at each corner.

Though streamlining was a '30s fad, the Airflow's styling failed to capture the public's imagination and it was this, as much as anything, which kept sales at low levels right up to the end in 1937. A more conventionally-styled version, the Airstream, was much more successful.

America's motor industry would be at the forefront of full-width styling when it returned with a vengeance in the 1940s, but American manufacturers would not wholeheartedly adopt unitary construction and aerodynamic shapes until the 1980s. The Airflow, combining all these innovations in the 1930s, was way ahead of its time.

1934 Chrysler Airflow	
Engine	5301cc 45-degree V16
Bore x stroke	82.6 x 123.8mm
Valvegear	Sidevalve
Fuel system	Single carburettor
Power	115bhp at 3400rpm
Suspension	Front: tubular beam axle with semi-elliptic leaf springs; rear: live axle with semi-elliptic springs
Wheels	16in steel disc wheels
Brakes	Hydraulic drum brakes all round
Top speed	90mph (145km/h)

Above and below: The 1930s Chrysler Airflow was way ahead of its time, with a modern-style pressed steel monocoque body which was shaped for good aerodynamic penetration.

Citroën Traction Avant

So advanced was the Citroën Traction Avant that it survived for more than two decades from its introduction in 1934. With front-wheel drive, a monocoque chassis/body, independent front suspension and dead beam rear axle, the Traction Avant set a pattern which would not be out of place on a modern saloon car.

It was launched at the 1934 Paris show, with a choice of 1303cc or 1529cc four-cylinder engines, later joined by a 1911cc unit. With the larger engine the 'Onze Legère' (Light Eleven), as it was later known, was good for 75mph (121km/h) and offered unmatched roadholding thanks to its front-wheel drive and the low centre of gravity afforded by the unitary body.

A six-cylinder Light 15 was offered from 1938, but production of all models was interrupted by the Second World War. The production lines were restarted at the end of the war, and the Traction Avant continued well after the introduction of Citroën's advanced DS in 1955. The last one of more than 759,000 Traction Avant cars was built in July 1957.

Citroën paid a heavy price for the Traction Avant's success. Development of the car bankrupted the company, and founder André Citroën was forced to sell to his biggest creditor, the Michelin tyre company, in 1935. He died of cancer the same year, and never saw the great success of the Traction Avant.

Above and below: The Traction Avant played every role, from family car, taxi and police car to elegant boulevard cruiser, as in this rare 'decapotable' (drophead) version.

Auburn 851 Speedster

Auburn was a long-established wagon manufacturer which turned its attention to cars early in the 20th century. By the 1920s it was ailing, with a line-up of unexciting products, but that changed with the appointment of E.L. Cord as general manager in 1924.

Cord injected pizzazz into Auburn's products, and the company enjoyed a revival. But Auburn's fortunes proved to be a rollercoaster ride of success and disaster, and by 1934 the prospects seemed grim. What the company needed, Cord reasoned, was a high-profile model to generate interest in the brand – but little capital was available to create that model.

Stylist Gordon Buehrig came up with the answer. His Auburn Speedster cleverly incorporated some existing, though reworked, panels into a fashionable new body design. The chassis was largely carried over from previous models, but the engine that powered the Speedster was new, a supercharged straight-eight built by Lycoming and said to develop 150bhp. Famous racing driver Ab Jenkins proved the car's potential by setting a US stock car record with a 12-hour run at over 100mph (161km/h), and production Speedsters carried a plaque bearing Jenkins' signature as a result.

The Speedster helped raise Auburn's profile, but most buyers opted for more practical – and cheaper – models. Even that couldn't save Auburn, which closed in 1936. About 600 Speedsters were built, and today they are highly prized.

1935 Auburn 851 Speedster	
Engine	4587cc Lycoming in-line eight
Bore x stroke	77.8 x 120.6mm
Valvegear	Pushrod-operated overhead valves
Fuel system	Single Stromberg carburettor plus centrifugal supercharger
Power	150bhp at 4000rpm
Suspension	Front: beam axle with semi-elliptic leaf springs; rear: live axle with semi-elliptic springs
Wheels	16in bolt-on wire wheels
Brakes	Drum brakes all round
Top speed	100mph (161km/h)

Below: Existing body panels were cleverly reworked by stylist Gordon Buehrig into a far more appealing design.

BMW 328

Austin's tiny Seven provided the basis for the very first BMW. Known as the Dixi, it was a licence-built Seven, but from these humble beginnings, BMW quickly blossomed into a serious manufacturer and branched out with increasingly confident designs of its own. By far the best known of its pre-war products was the amazing 328 sports car.

The flowing curves of its lightweight alloy body gave the good aerodynamic performance, aided by headlamps integrated into the bodywork and a swept-back radiator grille, carrying the twin 'kidney' apertures that were now a BMW hallmark. Underneath the skin the 328 was based around the best of previous BMWs, with a tubular chassis and and straight-six engine.

The engine was improved with the addition of a new light-alloy cylinder head with efficient hemispherical combustion chambers and opposed valves. The valves were still operated by the single, low-mounted camshaft, using conventional vertical pushrods and rockers for the intake valves and a second set of short, horizontal pushrods lying across the top of the engine to operate the exhaust valves. Three downdraught Solex carburettors fed the air/fuel mixture through vertical intake ports. This sophisticated 2.0-litre engine developed 80bhp, and in racing trim delivered up to 135bhp.

Above: The 328's driver looked out over a long, louvred bonnet under which sat a clever 'cross pushrod' engine of 2.0 litres developing 80bhp and giving sparkling performance.

Below: Flowing lines gave the 328's lightweight alloy body a stylish appearance and also gave it good aerodynamics. Note the fashionable exposed spare wheel in the tail.

The 328 made its public debut in Germany's Eifelrennen sports car race in 1936, where it won its class. Soon 328s were the car to have in sports car racing across Europe, to the point where 328s dominated sports car grids – filling the first four rows at the German Grand Prix meeting.

Works cars adopted more extreme streamlined roadster bodies for the Le Mans 24-hour race in 1938 and won their class. For the 1940 Mille Miglia the streamliner was even further developed, with a closed 'saloon' body built by Touring of Milan on their Superleggera principles, the idea being to reduce drag still further. BMW had been invited to send a team by Mille Miglia organiser Conte Aymo Maggi to ensure that his famed endurance event around Italy – which had been hit by tragic accidents and controversy – would be a proper 'international' race. Huschke von Hanstein and Walter Baumer won in their 328 saloon with more works BMWs third, fifth and sixth.

After the war 328s continued to be effective club competition cars, one notable 328 driver being a young Stirling Moss. And the powerful cross-pushrod engine would be further refined and developed by British maker Bristol to power its own range of cars, initially BMW-based, and would continue into the 1960s.

Above: The twin-aperture grille was already a feature of BMWs by the time the 328 arrived.

1937 BMW 328	
Engine 1971cc in-line six	
Bore x stroke 66 x 96mm	
Valvegear Pushrod ohv	
Fuel system Three Solex carburettors	
Power 79bhp at 5000rpm	
Suspension Front: independent, wishbones and transverse leaf spring; rear: live axle and semi-elliptic leaf springs	
Wheels 16in steel disc	
Brakes Hydraulic drum brakes all round	
Top speed 93mph (150km/h)	

Fiat 500 'Topolino'

Fiat's first 'people's car' was the 500, introduced in 1936. Its diminutive size and cheeky styling soon earned it the popular nickname 'Il Topolino' – the little mouse.

Dante Giacosa, who would be responsible for many a memorable Fiat over the next few decades, was responsible for the 500's simple engineering. Giacosa opted for a ladder chassis with its two channel-section side-members drilled to reduce weight. At the front he mounted an in-line four-cylinder sidevalve engine with an iron block and head, generating just 13bhp from its 569cc. A transverse leaf spring provided independent front suspension, while at the rear quarter-elliptic leaf springs carried a live axle.

Though it was cramped (early cars had only two seats), slow and noisy by car standards, the Topolino was a more comfortable and more practical mode of transport than a motorcycle combination. It provided essential transport for impecunious Italians, and quickly became as well-loved in its own market as the contemporary Austin Seven was in the UK.

After the war a revised 500B was introduced, the original 500 inevitably becoming known retrospectively as the 500A. The new car looked much the same, but under the bonnet it had a new overhead-valve engine, still displacing 569cc but now producing a heady 16.5bhp. It was little more than a stop-gap to a more heavily revised 500C, which followed in 1949. A full-width front end with integral headlamps modernised the Topolino, and in this form it remained in production until 1955.

Above: Dante Giacosa gave the 'Topolino' an all-iron four-cylinder engine of 569cc, developing 13bhp. It was conventionally mounted at the front of the car.

Below: The cheeky appearance of the compact Fiat 500 led to the 'Topolino' nickname, which means 'little mouse' in Italian. The 500 did for Italy what the Austin Seven did for Britain.

SS Jaguar 100

1937 SS Jaguar 100 3.5-litre
Engine 3485cc in-line six
Bore x stroke 82 x 110mm
Valvegear Pushrod-operated overhead valves
Fuel system Twin SU carburettors
Power 125bhp at 4250rpm
Suspension Front: beam axle with semi-elliptic leaf springs; rear: live axle with semi-elliptic springs
Wheels 18in knock-off wire wheels
Brakes Drum brakes all round
Top speed 100mph (161km/h)

Left: Wide, sweeping wings and big headlamps gave the SS Jaguar 100 a rakish appearance. William Lyons himself was responsible for the highly attractive styling. A new overhead-valve cylinder head by Weslake boosted the SS100's 2.7 litre engine to 102bhp, giving the new car sparkling performance to go with its looks.

Above: The cramped interior is typical of a vintage sports car, as is the comprehensive instrumentation. Weather protection was rudimentary at best.

William Lyons' Swallow company began building sidecars in 1922, and moved into cars with a special-bodied Austin Seven in 1927. By 1931 Lyons was ready to build a complete car of his own, the Standard-based SS1. The short-chassis SS90 which followed in 1935 was effectively a trial run for the SS100 a year later.

Like the earlier cars the SS Jaguar 100 had handsome lines penned by Lyons himself, with sweeping wings, cutaway doors, a folding screen and large headlamps. The big difference between them was under the bonnet. While the SS90 still used the Standard-based side-valve engine from the earlier cars, the SS100 had a new overhead valve cylinder head designed by engine expert Harry Weslake, boosting the 2.7-litre engine from 70bhp to 102bhp.

An even faster 125bhp 3.5-litre version was introduced in 1937 and it continued in production until war intervened. Both were immensely attractive and very fast, and together they did their job of raising the profile of SS in the years leading up to the Second World War. But SS concentrated on building their bread-and-butter machines, so production of the SS Jaguar 100 was never high – just 308 of all types.

The cars that would follow dropped the SS name in favour of Jaguar, which had been used as a model name since 1936 – and Jaguars would be among the most exciting classics of all.

MG T-series

MG enthusiasts had mixed feelings about the new TA-type Midget which replaced the PB in 1936. The P-type Midgets had been stiff-riding, uncompromising sports cars with sophisticated overhead-cam engines. The TA had all the good looks of its forebears and more power, but purists looked with dismay at the Morris-influenced engineering under the skin.

The TA was longer and wider than previous Midgets, which gave it a roomier cabin, more luggage space and a larger fuel tank but meant an increase in overall weight. To offset that, it was given a larger 1292cc engine producing 52bhp – though enthusiasts were disappointed to find that the new engine was a Morris side-valve unit rather than the Wolseley-engineered overhead-cam engines of previous cars. The suspension had been softened to improve the ride quality, and the TA boasted four-wheel hydraulic brakes. It was clearly a more refined and more mature car than any of the previous Midgets.

In 1939 the Midget was given a new engine and gearbox, turning it into the TB. Flying in the face of convention the new Morris M10 engine was slightly smaller than the unit it replaced at 1250cc, but it offered significant advantages. With a shorter stroke and wider bore than before it promised better reliability, and there was a small increase in power throughout the rev range. Another benefit was the new gearbox, which used the much closer ratios of the bigger MG VA. Sadly few were made before the outbreak of war.

Above: T-series styling gradually evolved over the years, but all the cars had separate wings and stand-up headlamps. This is the MG TD, introduced in 1948.

Below: Steel disc wheels were introduced on the TD, to howls of protest from enthusiasts who insisted that all proper sports cars should be fitted with wire wheels.

In 1945 MG unveiled the TC, little more than a mildly reworked TB with a slightly wider body. Yet it was the TC which would make MG a household name not just in Europe, but also in the USA. Of the 10,000 TCs made between 1945 and 1948, just over 2000 went Stateside, many with returning servicemen who marvelled at the sheer fun to be had from the little British sports car.

The car that replaced the TC – almost inevitably known as the TD – blended the TC's traditional body style with the accomplished chassis of the Y-type MG saloon of 1947. Independent front suspension gave the Y-type excellent road manners, which were continued in the TD. Not that all MG enthusiasts approved: modern disc wheels were standard for the first time on an MG sports car, and the purists derided them.

In 1953 the TD was facelifted to produce the attractive, but still olde-worlde, TF. New rivals from Triumph and Austin-Healey soon made the MG appear archaic. Greater performance from a 1.5-litre engine helped, but the TF still looked behind the times. It took until 1955 for a truly modern MG to appear, despite the seeds having been sown as early as 1951 with a rakish Le Mans special based on the TD.

Today the TF, last of the T-series line, is one of the most highly-prized and most valuable of all MG models – thanks largely to its suave looks, which seemed so outmoded when it was new.

Above: The double-humped scuttle and cutaway doors were characteristic features of all the T-series cars. The series continued until 1955, when the TF was replaced by the MGA.

MG TC 1945-49
Engine 1250cc in-line four
Bore x stroke 66.5 x 90mm
Valvegear Pushrod ohv
Fuel system Two SU carburettors
Power 54.4bhp at 5200rpm
Suspension Front: beam axle and semi-elliptic leaf springs; rear: live axle and semi-elliptic leaf springs
Wheels 17in wire-spoke
Brakes Hydraulic drum brakes all round
Top speed 78mph (125.5km/h)

Volkswagen Beetle

Ferdinand Porsche designed a people's car for Adolf Hitler in the 1930s, when it was known as the KdF-wagen (where KdF stood for Kraft durch Freude, 'strength through joy'). Serious production did not begin until after the war, by which time the Wolfsburg factory was under British control. British motor industry experts were shown the prototype car and expressed misgivings about the design, but they were proved wrong: the 'Beetle' went on to become the best selling car ever, eclipsing the Model T Ford.

The simple formula of the 'Type 1' was based on a pressed steel platform chassis, with an air-cooled flat-four engine mounted at the back. Early cars had split rear windows and a 1131cc engine, but numerous changes and improvements were made over the years. A bigger oval rear window arrived in 1953 and featured on the popular 1200 model introduced a year later. The rear window was changed again in 1958, this time to a rectangular shape. Bigger engines followed, a 1285cc unit in 1965 and a 1493cc, 44bhp engine in 1966.

The 'Super Beetle' of the 1970s introduced MacPherson strut front suspension, disc front brakes, a rounded nose providing more luggage space and the debut of a curved windscreen. Throughout the Beetle's career – which continued in South America after German production ended in 1980 – there was an attractive convertible option, and these are now the most sought-after Beetles of all.

Above: Ferdinand Porsche mounted the VW's air-cooled flat-four engine in the tail. Note the split rear window on this 1947 car.

Below: The 'Beetle' shape changed little over the years. It became familiar the world over, as the VW eclipsed the Ford Model T's sales record.

Jaguar XK120

Above: The Jaguar XK120's styling was fresh and new in 1948. The car caused a sensation when it was unveiled at the London Motor Show.

1949 Jaguar XK120
Engine 3442cc in-line six
Bore x stroke 83 x 106mm
Valvegear Twin overhead camshafts
Fuel system Twin SU carburettors
Power 160bhp at 5000rpm
Suspension Front: wishbone and torsion bar; rear: live axle with semi-elliptic springs
Wheels 16in wire or steel-disc wheels
Brakes Hydraulic drum brakes all round
Top speed 125mph (201km/h)

Jaguar caused a sensation at the first post-war London Motor Show in 1948. War-torn Britain was still suffering from rationing, and had just endured one of the coldest winters anyone could remember. Yet Jaguar's stand at the Earls Court show revealed a breathtaking new sports car, the XK120, which promised to deliver exceptional performance at a remarkably affordable price.

Its role was two-fold. First, the XK120 was a show-stopping attention-getter to raise Jaguar's profile as it introduced a series of important post-war saloon cars. Second, the XK120 allowed Jaguar to prove the all-new XK engine in a low-volume car before using it in a mainstream saloon.

The 3.4-litre XK engine was a classic in-line six-cylinder unit with twin overhead camshafts, said to develop 160bhp in its initial form. The car it powered was built on a chassis related to that of the new MkV saloon, but shorter and lighter, and at first clothed in aluminium alloy bodywork. Steel-bodied production cars came on stream in 1950.

The first XK120s were dropheads, but a fixed-head coupé was added to Jaguar's lineup in 1951, the same year that the competition-orientated XK120C (better known as the C-type) was revealed.

In 1954 Jaguar unveiled the XK140, a more powerful and better-handling vehicle but perhaps lacking a little of the XK120's styling purity. The XK150 of 1957 was even more a grand tourer, with more interior space, greater luxury and more power to offset increased weight.

The XK line continued until 1961, when it was replaced by another Jaguar sensation, the E-type.

Above left: As ever, William Lyons was personally involved in the XK120's styling. The shape was continued in the XK140 and XK150 models.

Above: The twin-cam XK engine, initially used in 3.4-litre form, would be used by Jaguar for decades to come.

Morris Minor

Alec Issigonis, who would later create the BMC Mini, was also the brains behind the Morris Minor. And given a freer hand the Minor could have been just as revolutionary: Issigonis' early plans included the use of front-wheel drive and a flat-four engine, but cost considerations forced the adoption of rear-wheel drive and an existing power unit, the 918cc side-valve engine from the Morris Eight Series E.

Even so, on its introduction in 1948 the Minor was a very modern design. The conventional separate chassis was gone, Issigonis combining the load-bearing members into the floor of the pressed-steel bodyshell in a 'unitary' structure. Issigonis designed the Minor with front-biased weight distribution, giving excellent stability in all conditions. Even the styling was innovative, with the headlamps set low in the front of the car.

Sadly new safety legislation forced Morris to raise the Minor's headlights in 1949. A four-door model followed in 1950, then the Series II cars appeared in 1952 with their 803cc Austin engines. In 1954 the 'cheesecutter' grille gave way to the more familiar horizontally-slatted type, and a new dashboard modernised the interior. The Morris 1000 of 1956 had the larger 948cc A-series engine, and a new single-piece curved windscreen – though, curiously, the Post Office Minor vans retained the old 803cc engine until the early 1960s. The millionth Minor was built in 1960, with a run of lilac-coloured 'Minor Millions' to celebrate. The last major update was the fitment of the 1098cc engine in 1962, after which the Minor soldiered on almost unchanged. Production of saloons ended in 1971, but the light commercials were still produced until 1974.

Above: Monocoque construction gave the Minor a spacious interior for a car its size.

Below: Excellent roadholding and stability made the Minor a safe and predictable car, but early models had minimal performance thanks to their aged side-valve engines.

Porsche 356

1960 Porsche 356 Super 90	
Engine 1582cc air-cooled flat-four	
Bore x stroke 82.5 x 74mm	
Valvegear Pushrod-operated overhead valves	
Fuel system Twin Zenith carburettors	
Power 90bhp at 5500rpm	
Suspension Front: trailing arms and torsion bars; rear: swing axles, radius arms and transverse torsion bars	
Wheels 15in steel wheels	
Brakes Hydraulic rum brakes all round	
Top speed 115mph (185km/h)	

Above left and above: The prototype 356, built in late 1947, looked similar to the production cars but was significantly different in its mechanical layout and structure.

Porsche started work on the first car to be marketed under its own name in 1947. The prototype 356 carried its 1131cc Volkswagen-based engine amidships in a tubular spaceframe chassis and was clothed in hand-beaten aluminium panels, but by the time serious production got under way in 1949 the design had been revised with a rear-mounted engine and a platform chassis carrying a pressed-steel body.

Early cars were built at Porsche's workshops in Gmünd, but production moved to Stuttgart in 1950. Gradually the 356 was developed, with ever larger engines, first a bored-out 1300 and then a long-stroke 1500 with a built-up roller-bearing crankshaft. In 1954 Porsche introduced the 356 Speedster which lacked some of the usual 356 equipment but was lighter, faster and also cheaper – inevitably it sold well. In 1955 numerous revisions were incorporated in the 356A.

The same year Porsche introduced a high performance version of the 356, known as the Carrera. The extra performance came from a 100bhp 1498cc engine with twin overhead camshafts per cylinder bank, an engine already a success in Porsche's 550/1500RS racing car.

Further revisions, including a taller and wider bodyshell, produced the 356B of 1958, powered by 1582cc engines with 60bhp, 75bhp or 90bhp. The last of the line was the 356C of 1963, with retuned suspension and all-round disc brakes. By then work was already under way on the 356's successor, the iconic 911.

Above: The simple dashboard of the Porsche 356 prototype presented only essential information to the driver. The car's white plastic steering wheel would hardly be considered 'sporting' today.

Jaguar C-type/D-type/XKSS

Fast though it was, the Jaguar XK120 was never likely to be a serious threat to the purpose-built Ferraris and Cunninghams in sports car racing. To meet the challenge Jaguar planned a lightweight racing machine with a sleek aluminium body, powered by a tuned XK engine. It was to be called the XK120C, 'C' for Competition, but soon became known as the Jaguar C-type.

Unlike the XK120 with its box-section steel chassis, the C-type used a very stiff tubular steel structure to form the centre of the car, with a lightweight subframe carrying the wishbone front suspension and the 200bhp twin-carburettor engine. The live rear axle was suspended by torsion bars and braking was by big drums front and rear.

The C-type made its Le Mans debut in 1951, where two of the three cars entered were sidelined with engine failures but the third, driven by Peter Walker and Peter Whitehead, won convincingly.

Jaguar put the C-type into limited production in 1952 and reappeared at Le Mans that year with special streamlined cars. But the low-drag bodywork led to engine overheating, which put the C-types out of the race. More successful was the debut of disc brakes on the C-types at the Mille Miglia, and in 1953 Jaguar was back at the front with C-types first, second and fourth at Le Mans.

A new car, the D-type, was readied for 1954. Like the C-type it was based around a stiff central structure, but instead of a tubular frame the D-type had a stressed-skin monocoque similar in concept to advanced aircraft designs. The

Below: The Jaguar XK120C or C-type was a purpose built sports racing car which built on the competition success of the XK120 road car, and continued such success at Le Mans.

Left: The driver, once installed in the D-type's snug cockpit, was reasonably well protected by a wrap-around plastic windscreen.

Above: Aerodynamicist Malcolm Sayer shaped the bodywork of the D-type Jaguar. Low drag, with the Le Mans' long Mulsanne straight in mind, was the aim.

Above: The XKSS was a road-going version of the D-type, with a road-car windscreen and hood. Just 16 were completed before the production line was destroyed by fire.

familiar XK engine was mounted at the front, now incorporating dry-sump lubrication to reduce the height of the tall unit and improve oil feed to the bearings in race conditions. With the long Mulsanne straight at Le Mans firmly in mind the new car was given a gorgeous low-drag body designed by aircraft aerodynamicist Malcolm Sayer.

The D-type could only manage second place on its Le Mans debut in 1954, but Mike Hawthorn and Ivor Bueb won in 1955 – though only after the Mercedes-Benz cars were withdrawn following the accident which killed Mercedes driver Pierre Levegh and 80 spectators. In 1956 the works cars failed but the Ecurie Ecosse team, using ex works D-types, came through to win and they repeated the success in 1957.

Earlier that year a major fire at Jaguar's Coventry factory had ended the career of a road-going derivative of the D-type, before it had really begun. The XKSS was intended to be the ultimate Jaguar road car, and also a useful tool for American production sports car racing. It was effectively a D-type with a full windscreen, tiny bumpers, indicators and a rudimentary hood. Just 16 were built before the fire destroyed the production line.

The C-type and D-type Jaguars are today some of the best-loved of all classic competition cars, and command enormous sums when they come up for sale – particularly those with interesting competition records. There's a whole industry based on building replicas, usually using later versions of the long-running XK engine rescued from a rusting XJ6 saloon. But there's nothing quite like the real thing.

1955 Jaguar D-type	
Engine	3442cc in-line four
Bore x stroke	83 x 106mm
Valvegear	Twin chain-driven overhead camshafts
Fuel system	Three twin-choke Weber carburettors
Power	285bhp at 5750rpm
Suspension	Front: wishbones and torsion bars; rear: live axle with trailing arms and torsion bars
Wheels	6.50-16in alloy
Brakes	Hydraulic disc brakes all round
Top speed	176mph (283km/h)

Austin-Healey 100

Donald Healey's Austin-based sports car, the Healey Hundred, was famously adopted by Austin overnight at the London Motor Show: it swiftly became the Austin-Healey 100.

Healey's clever re-use of rather mundane Austin mechanicals produced a tough, capable sports car that performed well but didn't cost the earth. The original 100, with a 2660cc four-cylinder engine from the woefully dull Austin Atlantic, was originally mated to an existing four-speed gearbox which had its too-low first gear blanked off to produce a three-speeder with reasonable ratios. Double overdrive also helped, and a proper four-speed (plus overdrive) 'box followed in 1955.

Higher performance versions of the Austin-Healey inevitably followed. The first of them was the 100M with a high-compression engine developing 110bhp. Even faster was the desirable 100S introduced in 1954, fitted with an alloy-head version of the Austin engine generating 132bhp, along with lightweight alloy panels and disc brakes. Just 55 100S models were built.

In 1956 the four-pot car was replaced by the six-cylinder 100/6 (which led to the earlier car being retrospectively referred to as the 100/4). Early 100/6s all offered two-plus-two accommodation, but the two-seater wasn't completely dead: a version was reintroduced in 1958. Though more refined than before the 100/6 was slower than the four-cylinder cars it replaced, a situation not rectified until the advent of the Austin-Healey 3000 in 1959.

1953 Austin-Healey 100

Engine 2660cc Austin in-line four

Bore x stroke 87.3 x 111.1mm

Valvegear Pushrod-operated overhead valves

Fuel system Twin SU carburettors

Power 90hp at 4000rpm

Suspension Front: wishbones, coil springs and anti-roll bar; rear: live axle with semi-elliptic springs

Wheels 16in wire wheels

Brakes Hydraulic drum brakes all round

Top speed 115mph (185km/h)

Chevrolet Corvette 1953-62

Though they pioneered a brand that's still going strong today, the first Corvettes were under-engineered, under-powered and unpopular. The idea was to provide a home-grown American answer to the influx of European sports cars, from the MGs and Triumphs at the bottom end to the Jaguar XK120 further uprange. Style was the major attraction, the glassfibre body penned by Harley Earl's team hitting every one of the 1950s dream-car hot spots from the wrap-around screen and cowled headlamps to the two-place cockpit and glitzy dashboard. Early cars had a prosaic 3.8-litre six with just 150bhp, but V8s soon came on stream to offer a small but welcome boost in performance.

For 1956 the Corvette was heavily restyled with four headlamps, scalloped sides and a twin-bulge bonnet aping the Mercedes-Benz 300SL. Under the skin there were big changes, too, with bigger V8 engines (up to 5.4 litres) offering as much as 360bhp. For the first time that gave the Corvette the straight-line speed to match its looks: the original straight-six cars could barely exceed 100mph (161km/h) but late '50s V8s were good for nearly 140mph (225km/h). Up against tidy-handling European opposition the Corvette's brakes and suspension were nothing to write home about, but careful development gradually improved the handling to the point where the Corvette became competitive in production sports car racing.

All Corvettes have a strong following, but for the most part they're available in reasonable numbers. Not so the early 1950s versions, and that rarity makes them the most valuable classic Corvettes of all.

Above: The first-generation Corvette is a fascinating piece of '50s nostalgia, though it was less popular than expected when it was new.

Below: Whitewall tyres and wrap-around windscreen point to the Corvette's 1950s origins. Early cars had pedestrian 3.8-litre six-cylinder engines with 150bhp.

Triumph TR2/3

Triumph revealed a prototype of a new sports car at the London Motor Show in 1952. Though that car, the 20TS, never made it into production a heavily revised version did, in 1953.

Called the TR2, it had a longer version of the 20TS's stub-tailed two-seater body and a ladder-frame chassis with wishbone and coil independent front suspension. It was powered by a linered-down version of the Standard Vanguard in-line four-cylinder engine, with a capacity of 1991cc. Fitted with twin carburettors it provided 90bhp. The result was a tough, reliable sports car with a reasonable turn of speed.

An improved version, the TR3, went on sale in 1955, and in 1956 front disc-brakes were specified – the first volume-production car to have them. Power rose to 100bhp for the TR3a of 1957, and the nose was restyled with a full-width grille. From 1959 there was the option of a 2138cc engine.

When the bigger Michelotti-styled TR4 of 1961 came along with its modern full-width styling and wind-up windows, that should have been the end of the road for the 'sidescreen' TR3a. But strong demand from the American market for the traditional TR led Triumph to reconsider, and an export-only version continued to be made into 1962, alongside the new car. This was later dubbed the TR3b.

These sidescreen TRs were a major success for Triumph, more than 80,000 of them finding buyers between 1953 and 1962. They're still fun to drive, and because the spares situation is good and there are some excellent Triumph clubs to help out if things go wrong, they make sound classic buys.

Above: *In 1956 the TR3 became the first volume-production car to be fitted with disc front brakes. The flush front grille differentiates the TR3 from the TR2.*

Below: *Triumph's head of engineering, Ken Richardson, took a modified TR2 to a record 124mph (199km/h) flying mile on the Jabbeke highway in Belgium in 1953. Even the standard car was good for over 100mph (161km/h).*

Ferrari 250GT/GTO

The first road-going Ferraris were built in the late 1940s, although they were thinly-disguised racing machines. It wasn't until the 250GT appeared in 1954 that the cars were built in appreciable numbers.

All the 250s used a 2953cc version of the V12 designed by Gioacchino Colombo, the '250' name referring to the (approximate) capacity of one cylinder. Early 250GTs had 200bhp and could reach 120mph (193km/h). The elegant touring bodies were by Pininfarina, which was already established as Ferrari's preferred bodywork designer.

The rare 250GT Tour de France, with a tuned engine giving up to 280bhp, followed in 1955 and cabriolet versions of the 250GT were available from the end of 1957. More significant was the introduction in 1959 of a short wheelbase version with 8in (200mm) chopped out of the middle of the car, stiffening the chassis and improving the handling. They were an effective weapon in production sports car racing.

In 1962 the long-wheelbase 250GT was discontinued and the short-wheelbase car turned into the more comfortable and better-equipped 250GT Berlinetta Lusso. Meanwhile, for racing, Ferrari produced a lighter, more aerodynamic version called the 250GTO. Just 39 of these fantastic machines were built, but Ferrari fans the world over recognise their curvaceous low-drag bodywork in an instant.

The touring 250GT Lusso was now producing 240bhp, while the racing GTO was up to 300bhp. In an effort to improve power still further the V12 was bored out from 73mm to 77mm, taking its capacity up to 3286cc. The result was the 275 series, which replaced the 250 in 1964.

Above and below: Ferraris were only produced in small numbers until the mid-1950s when the 250GT arrived. This is a rare 250GT Tour de France, with a tuned engine developing 280bhp. The 250 series continued until 1964.

Mercedes-Benz 300SL

Mercedes-Benz dominated European sports car racing in 1952, finishing second on its debut in the Mille Miglia and then winning at Le Mans, the Nürburgring and in the South American Carrera Panamericana. The successful car was a lightweight coupé designed by Rudolf Uhlenhaut, known internally as W194. It took its engine and suspension from the existing 300 saloon and mounted them in a lightweight spaceframe chassis, clothed in a wind-cheating alloy body. Conventional doors were impossible because of the chassis design, so lift-up 'gullwing' doors were provided instead. The world soon knew it as the 300SL, the letters standing for 'sports lightweight'.

For 1953 Uhlenhaut planned a series of improvements to the SL, including bigger wheels and tyres, a new form of swing-axle rear suspension and fuel injection for the 3.0-litre straight-six engine. But before the revised car could appear in competition Daimler-Benz management turned its focus away from sports cars to Formula 1 Grand Prix racing.

That might have been the end of the SL, had it not been for Austrian émigré Max Hoffman, importer of Mercedes-Benz cars to the US. Legend has it that Hoffman told Daimler-Benz management that if they built a road-going 300SL he could sell a thousand of them, and backed up his argument with a down-payment.

The production car used the new fuel-injected engine and a slightly longer version of the spaceframe chassis, but reverted to the conventional swing-axle rear suspension of the earlier racing SLs. It was also given a steel body with

Below: The 300SL Roadster was easier to drive and an easier machine to live with than its 'gullwing' coupé predecessor.

Left: 'Gullwing' doors were dictated by the shape of the spaceframe chassis. Modifications allowed conventional, but heavier, doors on the Roadster.

Above: The 300SL Roadster (left) and coupé are two of the most glamorous cars ever to wear the Mercedes-Benz star.

aluminium opening panels, resulting in a significant increase in weight. Racing SLs had been comfortably trimmed but the road car was even more luxurious, and was given a tilting steering wheel to aid entry and exit. The new car made its debut at the International Motor Sports Show in New York in January 1954.

Production began later that year and continued until 1957, by which time nearly 1400 examples of the 'gullwing' SL had been built. It was replaced by a 300SL Roadster, but the folding top and the conventional doors with their wind-down windows were just part of a package of changes which made the new version far easier to live with.

The spaceframe chassis was revised with lower sills to accommodate the normal doors, and extra bracing was introduced into the front bulkhead and above the transmission tunnel to restore the lost stiffness. Though the modifications were effective, they added about 220lb (100kg) to the weight of the car. Engine revisions produced an increase in power to compensate. Another significant change was the adoption of the low-pivot swing-axle design, which improved the Roadster's on-the-limit handling.

Nearly 1900 Roadsters were built between 1957 and 1963, alongside more than 25,000 of the much cheaper – but visually similar – 190SL. Both were replaced by another Uhlenhaut masterpiece, the 'Pagoda roof' 230SL of 1963. By then the 300SL had established itself as a favourite of the rich and famous: filmstars Tony Curtis and Sophia Loren, King Hussein of Jordan, comedian Tony Hancock and jazz pianist Oscar Peterson all had them. The 300SL was the car to be seen in.

Above: The 300SL's dramatic shape was largely the result of aerodynamic testing, a legacy of its origins as a sports-racing car. Even the 'eyebrows' over the wheelarches were functional, separating the airflow along the side of the car to help keep the windows clean in bad weather.

1954 Mercedes-Benz 300SL 'Gullwing'
Engine 2996cc in-line six
Bore x stroke 85 x 88mm
Valvegear Single chain-driven overhead camshaft
Fuel system Direct fuel injection
Power 215bhp at 5800rpm
Suspension Front: double wishbones, coil springs, telescopic dampers, anti-roll bar; rear: swing axle, coil springs, telescopic dampers
Wheels 5x15in steel disc
Brakes Hydraulic drum brakes all round
Top speed 161mph (259km/h)

Ford Thunderbird

Ford's answer to the Chevrolet Corvette was less a sports car, more a fast touring machine. 'A new high-spirited personal car that's at home on boulevard… or open road,' said a sales brochure at the time. The Thunderbird was first seen as a prototype at the Detroit Auto Show early in 1954, and production T-birds started to roll off the lines later that year.

V8 engines from the start ensured that the straight-line performance was better than the 'vette, whether you specified the 'Fordomatic' auto transmission or the three-speed manual with automatic overdrive. There was effectively only one body, an open two-door two-seater with a removable glassfibre hard top. A power-operated folding hood was a popular option.

For 1956 the spare wheel was mounted externally to improve boot space and the hard top was given 'porthole' side windows. The standard 292ci (4785cc) V8 was joined by a high-performance 312ci (5113cc) option. The T-bird was restyled for 1957 with a new grille, revised bumpers and bigger rear fins, and there was a rare supercharged engine option.

The last of these 'Little Birds' was built in December 1957. The car that replaced them was a bigger, four-seater machine with boxy styling which led to its nickname of 'squarebird'. Successive generations of T-birds just kept getting bigger and heavier – and further away from the concept that made the original such a classic. Ford acknowledged that fact with the introduction in 2002 of a new generation of Thunderbirds with throwback styling – which inevitably acquired the nickname 'retro bird'.

Above: The Thunderbird was Ford's answer to the Chevrolet Corvette. It was a fast tourer with impressive performance thanks to big V8 engines.

1955 Ford Thunderbird	
Engine 4786cc 90-degree Ford V8	
Bore x stroke 95.3x 83.8mm	
Valvegear Pushrod-operated overhead valves	
Fuel system Single Holley carburettor	
Power 198bhp at 4400rpm	
Suspension Front: wishbones, coil springs and anti-roll bar; rear: live axle with semi-elliptic springs	
Wheels 15in steel wheels	
Brakes Drum brakes all round, servo assisted	
Top speed 115mph (185km/h)	

Below: There was only one T-bird body, an open two-door with a removable glassfibre top. This early car lacks the porthole side windows that were added to the hardtop in 1956.

BMW 507

American importer extraordinaire Max Hoffman was behind the BMW 507. When the V8-engined 502 saloon was introduced in 1954, Hoffman suggested building a sports car around the new engine. He also introduced BMW to Count Albrecht von Goertz, a German designer now resident in the US.

Goertz designed two V8-engined cars for BMW, a handsome two-door model available in coupé and cabriolet forms known as the 503, and an aluminium-bodied sports car – the 507. Fitted with a 150bhp version of the 3.2-litre V8 and capable of nearly 140mph (225km/h), the 507 had the performance to justify the exotic looks Goertz had given it. The 507 had a litheness and elegance to its lines which contrasted sharply with the over-detailed, chrome-laden excesses of Detroit at the same time, and it reflected Goertz' belief that simplicity and restraint were the way to a timeless and effortlessly attractive shape.

Hoffman had told BMW he'd order 2000 507s provided that the purchase price would be 12,000 Deutschmarks. Sadly the 507 went on sale at nearly double that, which meant a US list price edging towards $9000 at its launch, and as a result a very limited clientele. Just 254 were built between 1957 and 1959, the last few with disc front brakes and even higher prices. Today that makes the 507 the rarest and most desirable BMW of its era, and one of the greatest 1950s classics of all.

Above and below: The clean, elegant lines of BMW's 507, by Count Albrecht von Goertz, were a refreshing change from the chrome clad excess offered by America's major manufacturers in the 1950s. Thanks to high prices the V8-engined 507 remained a rarity.

Lotus Elite

Racing car constructor Colin Chapman's first proper road car was true to Lotus' core values: light, agile, fast and technically advanced. Sadly it could also be fragile, and because of its higher cost of manufacture it wasn't the financial success that Chapman had hoped for.

The Elite was a monocoque design in an era when separate chassis were still common, but what made it even more unusual was that the entire body/chassis unit was made from glassfibre reinforced plastic. The spectacularly pretty styling, by John Frayling, was also very efficient aerodynamically. Suspension was all-independent, by wishbones and coils at the front and struts at the rear. Disc brakes were fitted all round, the rears inboard.

A race-derived all-alloy engine from Coventry-Climax provided the power, at first about 71bhp from just four cylinders and 1216cc. The 1960 Special Equipment model was tuned to give 85bhp and also had a close-ratio ZF gearbox. The Super 95, Super 100 and Super 105 models came in for further tuning, which increased power to as much as 105bhp.

It was a compelling package, though not always a reliable one. Quality control of the bodyshells was sometimes lacking (not least because Lotus chose cheaper suppliers over better ones) and the Coventry-Climax engine could be somewhat temperamental if maintenance was skipped.

In the end a little over a thousand Elites were sold. The model was replaced in 1963 by the Elan, which promised more performance and more reliability thanks to a steel backbone chassis and a bigger-capacity twin-cam engine based on Ford components – and also offered the option of a convertible body.

Above: The Elite's styling, by John Frayling, was deceptively simple but effortlessly beautiful. The body was a glassfibre monocoque. Coventry-Climax engines with up to 105bhp powered the Elites, and thanks to the suspension design know-how of Lotus boss Colin Chapman the handling and roadholding of these cars were unbeatable.

1963 Lotus Elite SE

Engine 1216cc in-line four

Bore x stroke 76.2 x 66.6mm

Valvegear Single chain-driven overhead camshaft

Fuel system Twin SU carburettors

Power 85bhp at 6300rpm

Suspension Front: wishbones, coil springs and anti-roll bar; rear: struts, fixed-length driveshaft links and radius arms

Wheels 15in wire wheels

Brakes Discs all round, inboard at rear

Top speed 118mph (190km/h)

Mini

The 1956 Suez Crisis led to the revival of interest in bubble cars, but BMC boss Leonard Lord had a better idea. Chief engineer Alec Issigonis was instructed to produce a proper small car, not a superannuated motorcycle combination. Lord's only stipulation was that Issigonis had to power the car with an existing BMC engine.

Only one engine was anything like suitable: the A-series unit which powered the Austin A35 and A40 Farina, and which had boosted the performance of the (Issigonis-designed) Morris Minor in the Minor 1000 of 1956. Issigonis mounted the engine sideways at the front of his new car, driving the front wheels through a gearbox which sat under the engine, sharing its oil supply. The resulting drivetrain was incredibly compact, which meant that the overall size of the car could be kept small while still offering useful interior space. Issigonis saved further space by badgering Dunlop to produce tiny 10in tyres.

At the 1959 launch the car was badged as the Morris Mini-Minor and the Austin Seven, but soon they were all just known as 'Minis' and the Austin and Morris badges were eventually dropped in 1969.

The Mini's excellent roadholding and handling were exploited to the full when racing car constructor John Cooper dropped a Formula Junior specification engine into one to produce the Mini-Cooper, an instant saloon car race winner and the most successful rally car of its era.

Despite regular reports of its imminent death, the Mini soldiered on and on, the last car being built in October 2000. More than five million were made.

1963 Morris Mini Cooper S	
Engine 1071cc in-line four, transversely mounted	
Bore x stroke 70.6 x 68.3mm	
Valvegear Pushrod-operated overhead valves	
Fuel system Twin SU carburettors	
Power 70bhp at 6000rpm	
Suspension Front: wishbones and rubber springs; rear: trailing arms and rubber springs	
Wheels 10in steel wheels	
Brakes Disc front, drum rear, servo assisted	
Top speed 95mph (153km/h)	

Below: The Mini's transverse engine, front-wheel drive layout set the pattern for small cars which endures today. The potent Mini-Cooper became a successful race and rally car.

Aston Martin DB4/5/6

T hese are the most influential Aston Martin models ever made. Their style and the strategy behind them has echoed down through the years, and still has a bearing on the products made by the very different Aston Martin company of today.

They stemmed from company owner David Brown's desire to take on – and beat – the best that Ferrari could offer. That meant building a car styled by the greatest designers in the world, and offering levels of performance greater than anything Aston Martin had previously produced.

Polish engineer Tadek Marek came to Aston Martin to design a new 3.7-litre six-cylinder engine, while Aston chassis engineer Harold Beach created a new steel platform chassis in consultation with the Carrozzeria Touring styling house. Touring penned a lithe and elegant fastback body to be built using their 'Superleggera' construction method where aluminium panels are supported by a lightweight tubular framework.

The DB4, as it was called, was launched at the London Motor Show in 1958. Though early cars were plagued by lubrication problems the DB4 was a huge success, selling faster than any previous Aston. Once the fixed-head coupé was in production a drophead was developed, and customers could specify more powerful 'Special Series' engines with three twin-choke Weber carburettors in place of the usual SUs.

Above: Tadek Marek's twin-cam straight-six engine, in various sizes and levels of tune, powered every one of the DB4/5/6 family of Aston Martins.

Below: The DB4 body was styled by Carrozzeria Touring and built using the company's Superleggera construction method, which proved both light in weight and elegant.

In 1960 a racing derivative, the DB4 GT, was introduced. With a five-inch shorter wheelbase, just two seats, and a tuned twin plug engine the DB4 GT proved to be a handsome and effective sports racing machine. Even more handsome, to many eyes, was the rare Zagato-bodied version which was lighter and even quicker.

A revised version of the DB4's chassis and an enlarged 4.0-litre version of its engine went into a new Lagonda, the Rapide, in 1961. In 1963 the revised engine found its way back into the Aston, which now incorporated numerous tweaks and improvements and was known as the DB5. The prototype DB5 (actually a late DB4 Vantage) was one of two cars used in the James Bond film *Goldfinger*, presenting Aston Martin with huge publicity in 1965.

By then Aston Martin was already planning to introduce a further revision of the same car, the DB6. Though this looked bigger and heavier than the DB5 there was actually little to choose between them: it was an optical illusion caused by the DB6's higher roofline, which gave more headroom to rear seat passengers. The DB6 continued until the end of 1970, latterly running alongside the new Aston Martin DBS and DBS V8 models.

1963 Aston Martin DB5	
Engine	3995cc in-line six
Bore x stroke	96 x 92mm
Valvegear	Twin chain-driven overhead camshafts
Fuel system	Three SU carburettors
Power	282bhp at 5500rpm
Suspension	Front: wishbones and coil springs and anti-roll bar; rear: coil-sprung live axle with trailing arms and Watts linkage
Wheels	15in wire wheels
Brakes	Hydraulic disc brakes all round, servo assisted
Top speed	143mph (230km/h)

Above left: 'Volante' had long been the name associated with open-top Astons, but the drophead DB5 is correctly called a DB5 Convertible.

Below: The higher roofline of the DB6 improved headroom in the rear, while the reshaped tail improved stability at speed.

Sunbeam Alpine/Tiger

The Alpine name, dormant since 1955, reappeared on a new two-seater sports car in 1959. The monocoque body shared its floorpan with nothing more exciting than the Hillman Husky, a utilitarian Minx derivative. But the styling was sharp (with prominent fins on early cars) and there was a twin-carb 1494cc to provide reasonable performance. In 1960 the Alpine was upgraded with a 1592cc engine, and the following year a fastback coupé version built by Harrington was approved by Sunbeam's parent company Rootes as an official model. Three distinct types were offered between 1961 and 1963, all of them rare.

In 1963 a host of detail improvements were made to the Alpine including revised suspension, better seats, quarter lights and an optional hardtop. The fins were trimmed in 1964, and the final cars built from 1965 to 1968 gained a 1725cc twin-carb engine with 92.5bhp.

If you wanted more power than that, you needed a Sunbeam Tiger – effectively an Alpine fitted with a 260ci (4261cc) Ford V8 engine developing 164bhp, turning it into a 120mph (193km/h) motor car. The Tiger II of 1967 offered even more pace, thanks to a larger 289ci (4727cc) Ford Mustang engine with 200bhp. But the Tiger was killed off in its prime, in 1968, after Rootes was taken over by the American Chrysler company. Chrysler objected to the use of a Ford engine in one of its products, and Chrysler's own V8 wouldn't fit.

Both the Alpine and Tiger are underrated cars, lacking the image of flashier MG, Triumph and Austin-Healey rivals. As classic sports cars go, they're bargains.

Above: *Comfortable interiors were a feature of both the Alpine and the V8-engined Tiger.*

Below: *Until 1964 Alpines had pronounced fins at the rear, as was then the fashion. They were toned down on later cars.*

Lincoln Continental

dsel Ford's Lincoln Continental was phased out in the late 1940s, but the Continental name reappeared as a marque in its own right in 1955. The Continental MkII was a vast, hand-built coupé with a $10,000 asking price, despite which Ford reputedly lost $1000 on each one. The next generation were lower-priced and in 1959 the Continental became a Lincoln again, but remained one of America's biggest and most flamboyant cars.

For 1961 a brand new and very different Continental was offered. Here was proof that less is, indeed, more: the new car was smaller and less ostentatious, with classic clean-cut styling that was the antithesis of the baroque excesses that it replaced. Just two models were available, a four-door saloon and a four-door convertible, both with forward-opening 'suicide' rear doors. A more than adequate 300bhp was provided by a 7.0 litre V8 engine driving the rear wheels through standard automatic transmission. In 1964 a long-wheelbase version was unveiled and in 1966 an even larger 7.6-litre V8 giving 365bhp was installed.

The Continental proved to be just the kind of luxury saloon upmarket buyers wanted in the 1960s, and more than 340,000 were built between 1961 and 1969. For several years the White House used Continentals as official cars – John F Kennedy was assassinated in his – while another appeared as crime boss transport in the film *Goldfinger*. American audiences were horrified when a real Continental (less its engine) was craned into a crusher and cubed...

Above: The convertible version of the '61 Lincoln Continental was a four-door car, like the saloon. The powered hood folded back effortlessly leaving an uncluttered rear deck.

Below: The Continental was one of America's most prestigious cars – so when a real car was crushed in the James Bond film Goldfinger, audiences were aghast.

Jaguar E-type

The E-type is an icon of the Swinging Sixties, and it isn't difficult to see why. Sensational looks, the ability to reach close to 150mph (241km/h), and all for half the price of an Aston or a Ferrari: Jaguar's sports car was an instant sensation.

Its curvaceous good looks – equally good in roadster and fixed-head forms – were clearly related to the Le Mans-winning D-types of the 1950s, sculpted by aerodynamicist Malcolm Sayer. Its structure was similar too, with a monocoque central tub and a tubular front section carrying the engine and front wheels – though the exotic aluminium and magnesium alloys of the D-type were replaced by steel. The E-type's engine was also shared with previous models, a 3.8-litre development of the fine straight-six XK unit with a claimed 265bhp. Wishbones and torsion bars provided independent suspension at the front, and the rear was also independently suspended by lower wishbones, fixed-length driveshafts and twin coil spring/damper units.

Jaguar claimed a top speed of 150mph (241km/h), which road tests subsequently proved – though the test cars had been carefully prepared and, in truth, production cars fell slightly short of the mark. Although production E-types weren't quite as quick, they were still as rapid as almost any competitor and much cheaper than most. The model soon became a regular in sports car racing, and Jaguar built a short run of lightweight E-types which are now highly prized.

Above: The familiar XK engine, a straight-six with twin overhead camshafts, provided the motive power for the E-type. This 3.8-litre engine is fed by three SU carburettors.

Below: The Series 1 fixed-head coupé is perhaps the best looking of all E-types – and surely one of the most admired classic cars of all.

A better gearbox and a torquier, 4.2-litre engine were introduced in 1964, and a two-plus-two coupé followed in 1966. Nine inches longer than the two-seater and an inch and a half taller, the two-plus-two was oddly proportioned – giving it an ungainly appearance.

Numerous small changes were implemented in what became known as the 'Series One and a Half', including a change to open, sealed beam headlamps, before the Series II proper was unveiled in 1968. The headlamps had been moved forward slightly and bigger indicators fitted, and the air intake had been enlarged to admit cooling air for the new optional air conditioning. Inside rocker switches replaced protruding toggle switches.

By the end of the 1960s increasingly stringent emissions rules in the US meant that a 'Federal' E-type produced just 177bhp. More power was a priority, and it came from a brand new V12 engine designed by Walter Hassan and Harry Mundy. In American specification the V12 offered a genuine 250bhp, despite lacking the fuel injection system originally planned – instead it was fuelled by a quartet of Zenith Stromberg carbs, and sparked by Lucas Opus electronic ignition. The V12 Series III E-type of 1971 used the longer wheelbase of the old two-plus-two car, with flared wheel arches, wider wheels and a new flush grille.

In the US the Huffaker Engineering and Group 44's Bob Tullius built successful racing machines based on Series III E-types, but even so the basic design was being overtaken by more modern rivals. The final E-types were sold in 1975. Jaguar never directly replaced the model, instead introducing a more refined and luxurious GT car, the XJ-S.

Thanks to its stunning looks and still-impressive performance, the E-type is a favourite among classic car enthusiasts the world over.

Above: The E-type's luscious curves derived from the aerodynamically shaped D-type racing car of the 1950s. The huge, tip-forward bonnet was a complex and expensive structure – and sadly, an easy one to damage through an ill-judged parking manoeuvre.

1961 Jaguar E-type

Engine 3781cc in-line six

Bore x stroke 87 x 106mm

Valvegear Twin chain-driven overhead camshafts

Fuel system Three SU carburettors

Power 265bhp at 5500rpm

Suspension Front: wishbones, torsion bars, and anti-roll bar; rear: independent with lower wishbone, radius arms, twin coil-spring/damper units and anti-roll bar

Wheels 15in wire wheels

Brakes Hydraulic disc brakes all round, servo assisted

Top speed 149mph (240km/h)

Mercedes-Benz 300SE/280SE 3.5

The mid-range Mercedes-Benz 'fintail' saloons of 1959 were joined by very elegant four-seater coupés and convertibles in 1961. At first there was just one engine, the fuel-injected 2195cc six with 120bhp, but in 1962 Mercedes-Benz topped off the saloon, coupé and cabriolet ranges with a 2996cc, 170bhp six with a choice of manual or automatic gearboxes. Disc brakes were fitted all round and the cars were equipped with air suspension derived from that in the 600 limousine. These 300SE models were twice the price of the 220SE, so inevitably production was limited.

A new range of W108 saloons appeared in 1965 and the fintail saloons were phased out, but the coupé and cabriolet models remained in production. The new 2496cc seven-bearing straight-six engine from the W108 250SE saloon was fitted from 1965 to 1968, and then the 2778cc 280SE engine took over until 1971. Both cars were fitted with all-disc brakes and the latest development of the Mercedes swing-axle rear suspension, while power assisted steering and an automatic gearbox were options.

The most exciting car in this revised range came in 1969, when Mercedes' new 3.5-litre V8 engine (also used in the long-wheelbase W109 saloon and soon destined for the SL sports car) was fitted to produce the confusingly named 280SE 3.5. With 200bhp on tap, the V8-engined cars were capable of 125mph (201km/h).

Few cars can match the elegance of these 1960s coupés and convertibles, and even fewer can remain unruffled while providing the kind of performance available thanks to the efficient Mercedes straight-six and V8 engines. It's no wonder that these remain some of the most sought-after post-war Mercedes-Benz models of all.

Above: The Mercedes-Benz coupés and cabriolets of the 1960s had clean, elegant lines with a timeless quality. Potent engines gave them a fair turn of speed, too. This is a 280SE.

1962 Mercedes-Benz 300SE	
Engine	2996cc in-line six
Bore x stroke	85 x 88mm
Valvegear	Single overhead camshaft
Fuel system	Bosch fuel injection
Power	157bhp at 5000rpm
Suspension	Front: double wishbones with air springs and anti-roll bar; rear: swing axles with air springs and anti-roll bar
Wheels	5.5 x 13in steel wheels
Brakes	Disc brakes all round
Top speed	109mph (175km/h)

Triumph TR4/5/6

Triumph's 'sidescreen' TRs proved popular, but by the end of the 1950s their styling was looking old fashioned. Italian stylist Michelotti was contracted to rework the TR3a, and he came up with an attractive full-width body with prominent headlamps. The TR4 carried forward fundamentally the same chassis, with minor improvements such as servo brakes and rack and pinion steering. A 2138cc engine was standard, providing 100bhp, which rose to 104bhp in the TR4a of 1964. More importantly the TR4a gained semi-trailing arm independent rear suspension, which improved the car's ride quality and ensured that it retained grip even on bumpy roads.

In 1967 the four-cylinder engine was replaced by a 2.5-litre straight-six for the 150bhp TR5, the first British car with fuel injection. Sadly the injected engine could not meet stringent American emissions regulations, so the US got twin Stromberg carburettors and a much less exciting output of 104bhp. The triple 'go-faster' stripe across the bonnet was little consolation.

For 1969 Karmann restyled the front and rear (but left the middle of the car alone to minimise re-tooling costs) to produce the TR6, but the chassis and engines remained much the same as before. The fuel injected cars were slightly detuned in 1972 with the fitment of a milder camshaft, but most of the quoted 25bhp power drop was accounted for by a difference in measurement standards. Three quarters of the TR6s produced were US-spec carburettored cars, which continued in production until 1976.

Above: Michelotti created a brand new body for the Triumph TR4 of 1961, but the mechanicals underneath the new model were largely those of the outgoing TR3a.

Below: A fuel-injected straight-six engine gave the TR5 plenty of smooth power. Sadly North American customers had to make do with the much less powerful carburettor-fed TR250.

AC Shelby Cobra

Some cars are created through the vision of a single-minded individual, but the Cobra's genesis was more tortuous. The story began with a twin-tube chassis designed for club racing by John Tojiero and featuring all-independent suspension with a transverse leaf-spring at the rear. In 1952 Cliff Davis had fitted one of these chassis with a 2.0-litre Bristol engine and a very pretty alloy body inspired by a Ferrari 166 Barchetta. The car came to the attention of Charles Hurlock of AC, who bought the car and decided to put it into production. The AC Ace was born, in 1954.

AC fitted its own overhead-cam 2.0-litre engine which gave 85bhp in triple-carburettor form, then offered Bristol engines as an option from 1956. When Bristol moved to Chrysler V8 power, AC looked around for an alternative and settled on tuned 2.6-litre Ford Zephyr engines.

Meanwhile, American race driver and engineer Carroll Shelby had come up with the idea of installing a powerful American V8 engine in a neat-handling European sports car chassis. As a driver Shelby had won at Le Mans for Aston Martin in 1959, and he went to his old team with the idea. Aston Martin showed interest but had other priorities, so Shelby approached AC with backing from Ford's Walter Hayes for supplies of Ford's new V8 engine. In the autumn of 1962 the first Cobra was built, Shelby dropping a 260ci (4261cc) Ford V8 into a mildly revised Ace chassis.

Top and above: *American Ford V8 power turned AC's pretty Ace into the scorching Cobra. Comprehensive instrumentation kept the driver in touch with the engine's health.*

Below: *Serious straight-line performance was a Cobra speciality, but the twin-tube chassis was really overwhelmed by the engine's power. Later cars had a redesigned chassis.*

The addition of V8 power made the Cobra extraordinarily fast – the sprint from rest to 100mph (161km/h) took just 14 seconds, still a more than respectable figure today. The chassis struggled to cope with the V8 power, but the Cobra was destined to become even more powerful. For 1963 the engine was upgraded to a 4.7-litre (289ci) unit, which could propel this Mk2 Cobra from rest to 60mph (97km/h) in less than six seconds and go on to 138mph (222km/h). The Cobra became a force in sports car racing, as well as an adrenaline-producing road car. At first only available in the US, it went on sale in Britain in right-hand drive form in 1964. That same year special Cobra coupés won the GT category at the Le Mans 24-hour race.

With Ford's help the Cobra chassis was completely redesigned for 1965. The new chassis was wider and stiffer, and it was fitted with more sophisticated coil and wishbone suspension all round (replacing the transverse leaf rear-end inherited from the Ace). Halibrand centre-lock alloy wheels were fitted and the bodywork revised with the addition of bulbous extended arches to cover the fat tyres. Powering this new Cobra was an even larger engine, the famous 427ci (6997cc) V8 which Ford had developed for NASCAR racing and which would power the Mk2 GT40s to victory at Le Mans in 1966. Cobra production continued until 1967, the last few built with the slightly larger but cheaper and less powerful Ford 428ci (7014cc) V8 engine.

The Cobra reappeared in 1983, initially as the 'AC MkIV', but Ford granted permission to use the Cobra name again in 1986. Today a revitalised AC produces MkV cars with modern engines. The Cobra legend continues…

Above: Early Cobras lacked the bulbous arches introduced later to cover vast Halibrand alloy wheels and wide tyres. Performance steadily increased as ever larger engines were fitted, culminating in a monstrous 7.0-litre V8 with more than 400bhp.

1965 AC Shelby Cobra 427
Engine 6997cc V8
Bore x stroke 107.7 x 96mm
Valvegear Pushrod overhead valve
Fuel system Two Holley carburettors
Power 410bhp at 6000rpm
Suspension Front: wishbones, coil springs; rear: wishbones, coil springs
Wheels Halibrand 15in alloy wheels
Brakes Hydraulic disc brakes all round, servo assisted
Top speed 165mph (266km/h)

Lotus Elan/+2

ey features of the Elan, new in 1962, were the chassis and engine. Unlike the glassfibre monocoque Elite that it replaced, the Elan had an unstressed glassfibre body mounted on a pressed-steel backbone chassis, forked at either end to provide engine and suspension mounting points. Disc brakes and all-round independent suspension – the latter developed with Lotus' usual flair – meant the chassis could cope with plenty of power.

To provide it, Lotus boss Colin Chapman came up with a plan for a new engine to replace the expensive and temperamental Coventry Climax unit in the Elite. Chapman hired Harry Mundy to design a twin-cam conversion for Ford's new Cortina engine, and sold Ford the idea of using the twin-cam powerplant both for his Elan and for a high-performance saloon (which became the Lotus-Cortina). Early engines were 1498cc but most were 1558cc, giving 106bhp from the start and up to 126bhp by the early 1970s.

By then the two-seater Elan – available in hardtop coupé and roadster forms – had been joined by a longer, wider two-plus-two coupé called the Elan +2. Though the +2 wasn't quite as crisp to drive as the two-seater Elan, the extra space was useful and it could still cover the ground quicker than almost anything else.

The Elan continued until 1973, the last of them in big-valve Sprint form with two-tone paint (commonly red over white with gold stripes, Team Lotus' Gold Leaf sponsor colours) and a very few with five-speed gearboxes. The +2 lasted little longer, being replaced by the bigger and faster Elite in 1974.

Above: Lotus followed the glassfibre monocoque Elite with the Elan, based on a pressed-steel backbone chassis. This is the later Elan +2, which offered two-plus-two accommodation.

Below: All the Elans were exceptional driver's cars, with excellent grip and phenomenal balance. Power came from various versions of the Lotus-Ford twin-cam engine.

MG MGB/MGC

MG's new monocoque sports car for 1962 was another home-grown success for Abingdon. It boasted more power than the outgoing MGA thanks to a bigger (1798cc) three-bearing engine, a higher axle ratio for more refined cruising on Britain's newly-constructed motorways, and front discs in case of emergency. A handsome fastback coupé, called the MGB GT, was added to the range in 1965 bringing with it a five-bearing engine and a quieter axle, which were adopted on the roadster in 1967.

The same year a new six-cylinder engine was squeezed under the bonnet (necessitating a compact new front suspension system with torsion bars) to produce the MGC and MGC GT. The heavy engine made the handling disappointing and it couldn't match the now-defunct Austin-Healey 3000 for performance (though two works MGC racing cars showed some potential) so the C was relatively unsuccessful.

Far better was the MGB GT V8, using the lightweight all-alloy Rover V8 engine. It was fast and handled tidily, but sold in lower numbers than the MGC had done. That rarity makes it a sought-after classic today.

Black polyurethane bumpers were adopted in 1974, along with an increase in ride height, to meet new North American safety requirements, but the handling suffered. Meanwhile power outputs continued to drop on export cars as emissions controls tightened. The MGB soldiered on, with little real development, until 1980.

But that wasn't quite the end of the road for the MGB. It was briefly revived by Rover in 1992 as the MG RV8, which remains rare and collectable.

Top: Many MGBs are modified to suit owners' tastes: this car has a non-standard wood-rim steering wheel.

Above and below: The MGB is one of the world's best-loved sports cars – tough and reliable, easy to work on, stylish and fun to drive. Those who yearn for more performance can choose the six-cylinder MGC or the MGB V8.

Triumph Spitfire/GT6

Triumph created one of the most popular of all small sports cars in 1962. The Spitfire was based on the chassis of the 1959 Herald saloon, with a curvy two-seater body by Michelotti, an 1147cc twin-carb engine with 63bhp and disc front brakes. Overdrive, wire wheels and a removable hardtop were soon added to the options list, and from 1965 there was a MkII version with more power (now 67bhp) and better trim.

The GT6 – a Spitfire with a fixed, fastback roofline and 2.0-litre straight-six engine – was added to the range in 1966. The following year the MkIII Spitfire was introduced with a higher front bumper to meet new North American requirements. More importantly there was now a 1296cc engine under the bonnet delivering 75bhp, and bigger front brake calipers. The GT6 adopted the new nose and revised rear suspension the following year.

The styling was tidied up by Michelotti for the MkIV Spitfire and MkIII GT6 of 1970, integrating the high-mounted bumper more neatly into the nose and introducing a new one-piece bumper/wings panel. The rear end was also reworked to echo the styling of the new Stag and MkII Triumph 2000. At the same time the gearing was raised and the swing-axle rear suspension revised.

The GT6 was dropped in 1973, while US-market Spitfires received bigger 1493cc engines, and in late 1974 that engine was made available to home-market buyers in the Spitfire 1500. Though the 71bhp power output was less than the MkIII had boasted back in '67 the 1500 was the most numerous of all Spitfires: nearly 96,000 were made before production ended in 1980.

Above: The low bumper of the original Spitfire was raised in 1967 to meet new North American regulations. The nose would be revised again in 1970 to neaten up the appearance.

Below: The Spitfire cleverly used Triumph Herald components to produce a compact, good-value sports car. For two decades it was the arch-enemy of the MG Midget/Austin-Healey Sprite. A GT6 coupé, with a fastback rear end and six-cylinder engine, was available from 1966.

Chevrolet Corvette Sting Ray

A new generation Corvette was unveiled for 1963, with a new box-section chassis on a slightly shorter wheelbase and all-independent suspension. The 250bhp, 327ci (5358cc) V8 engine was carried over from the previous generation Corvette. But the biggest news was the new car's outrageous styling, which had clear influences from Chevrolet's 1958 Stingray racing car and the 1959 XP-720 concept car, both styled by Bill Mitchell who had now taken over from Harley Earl as GM's design boss.

The outlandish shape of the Sting Ray – still in glassfibre, as with previous generations – had boldly curved wings with a hint of Jaguar E-type about them, concealed headlamps and dummy air ducts in the front wings. Previous Corvettes had all been roadsters, but the new car was available either as an open two-seater or as a rakish fastback coupé, with a controversial split rear window. Although the split window made for a more dramatic and cohesive shape it lasted only until 1964 when a conventional rear window was substituted, and some early cars were modified to the later style. But today it is the early cars which are more sought-after, and many a later Corvette has been given the early style window…

In 1965 Chevrolet introduced a new all-disc braking system and a 396ci (6489cc) V8 engine, and in 1966 an even more powerful 427ci (6997cc) V8 appeared. The Sting Ray was offered until 1967, and when a new Corvette appeared for '68 it would drop the 'Sting Ray' name – but it would reappear, as one word, for 1969.

Above: *Bill Mitchell's original Corvette Sting Ray was given a controversial split rear window – though it lasted just one season, it's now a sought-after feature.*

1963 Chevrolet Corvette Sting Ray	
Engine 5416cc 90-degree V8	
Bore x stroke 101.6 x 83.5mm	
Valvegear Pushrod-operated overhead valves	
Fuel system Rochester fuel injection	
Power 360bhp at 6000rpm	
Suspension Front: wishbones, coil springs and anti-roll bar; rear: wishbones, driveshaft links and transverse leaf spring	
Wheels 15in alloy wheels	
Brakes Drum brakes all round, servo assisted	
Top speed 150mph (241km/h)	

Ford Lotus-Cortina

Lotus boss Colin Chapman came up with the idea of building a new twin-cam engine, then slotting the result into both his own Elan sports car and a new high-performance saloon. That saloon was the Lotus-Cortina.

The twin-cam conversion designed by Harry Mundy, plus a small increase in capacity, boosted the basic Cortina engine from 60bhp to 105bhp. Chapman's attentions to the Cortina included coil springs and A-frame location for the rear axle, wider wheels and a distinctive livery – all the cars were white with a green flash.

Few other cars of the era offered sports-car performance with four-seat saloon accommodation, and the Lotus-Cortina quickly became an enthusiasts' favourite. It was also a spectacularly successful machine for saloon car racing, particularly in the hands of Jim Clark.

But it wasn't perfect. The A-frame locating the rear axle mounted on the differential casing, and the loads it fed into the axle caused the casing to distort, resulting in oil leaks. It wasn't uncommon to see a racing Lotus-Cortina trailing oil smoke from the rear. From 1966 it reverted to the leaf sprung live axle used on the softer Cortina GT to solve the problem.

In 1967 Ford launched a new Cortina. Though there was a twin-cam model (at first called the Cortina Lotus, later Cortina Twin Cam) it was not the drivers' car the previous model had been, and today it's the Mark 1 Lotus-Cortina which enthusiasts still lust after.

Above: Comprehensive instrumentation and a Lotus three-spoke steering wheel marked out the Lotus-Cortina's interior.

Below: All production Lotus-Cortinas were two-door saloons, in white with a green flash. This car is prepared for historic saloon car racing, which is more popular than ever.

Mercedes-Benz 230SL/250SL/280SL

In 1963 Mercedes-Benz introduced a single car to replace the mass-market 190SL roadster and the fast, expensive 300SL. The 230SL's clean, angular lines were first seen at the Geneva Salon in March 1963. The elegant hard top, which dipped towards the centre, gave the new SL its 'Pagoda roof' nickname.

The new car was based on the running gear of the W110/111 'Fintail' saloons which had been introduced at the end of the 1950s, and the new SL sports car carried over the saloon's double wishbone front and swing axle rear suspension. Though much shorter than the Fintail, the SL kept the wide saloon track front and rear, which helped provide it with excellent roadholding.

The engine was a development of the M127 unit which had already won a reputation for smoothness and flexibility in the Fintail saloons. For the SL, the M127 engine was bored out 2mm to 82mm, increasing the capacity to 2306cc. A new fuel injection system was fitted, and the engine delivered 150bhp at 5500rpm.

The 2.3-litre unit had to be revved hard to make the most of its power. To improve drivability a longer-stroke 2.5-litre engine (the M129) was fitted in 1967, giving the newly-named 250SL no more power than before but considerably more mid-range torque.

The 280SL of 1968 had even more capacity (2778cc) and even more power (now up to 170bhp). It remained in production until 1971, when Mercedes-Benz announced its replacement, the R107 350SL.

Top and above: A 2.8-litre six-cylinder engine with 170bhp made the 280SL the quickest of the 'Pagoda roof' SLs.

Below: Saloon car comfort and faultless build quality were major attractions of the SLs. Power steering and automatic transmission made them easy to drive.

Porsche 911

The early 1960s saw the Porsche 356 nearing the end of its development. The air-cooled flat-four engine had been extended from 1.1 litres to a full 2.0 litres and the bodywork had been enlarged and reshaped to improve passenger space, but Porsche wanted something even bigger and faster. A new car with a new engine was necessary, and it arrived in 1964.

The new design retained the 356's basic layout, mounting an air-cooled, horizontally-opposed engine behind the rear axle line. But the engine was all-new, a 130bhp six-cylinder unit with a single overhead camshaft on each cylinder bank. The suspension, however, was very different: at the front the 356's trailing arms gave way to more compact torsion-sprung struts, and at the rear the tricky swing axles were replaced by semi-trailing arms. The new car was longer so that it could offer more interior space, and was given a distinctive shape by Ferdinand Alexander Porsche.

Porsche called its new machine the 901, until Peugeot objected. The French company had long used three-digit numbers with a central zero for its own cars, so Porsche renamed its new model the 911, and an icon was born.

Early on the 911 proved to be unstable in a straight line, and in corners it generated strong initial understeer and violent lift-off oversteer. And it handled differently in left- and right-hand corners. Some examples were worse than others, and the cause was traced to production variations which upset the suspension geometry. A quick fix was to insert an 24lb (11kg) cast-iron weight

Below: The 911 took over from the 356 in 1964, offering more interior space and greater performance than its predecessor. It became an iconic sports car.

Above: F.A. 'Butzi' Porsche designed the 911's clean and well-proportioned fastback shape. Attractive alloy wheels were a popular option, standard on faster versions.

Above: The 911's flat-six engine began at 2.0 litres and was progressively enlarged. Note the large fan at the rear which draws air over the air-cooled engine.

into each end of the front bumper, to make the weight distribution less rear-biased and to increase the polar moment of inertia, making the 911 stable in corners.

Another problem was a flat spot in the middle of the rev-range. The solution was to ditch the special triple-barrel Solex carbs originally fitted to 911s in favour of triple-choke Weber carbs which had originally been designed for Lancia V6 engines.

Early cars were all fixed-head coupés, but in 1965 Porsche introduced an open-top 911 with a substantial fixed roll-over hoop, a removable roof section and a drop-down rear window (though this was quickly changed to a fixed, wrap-around rear screen). Porsche called it a 'Targa' top, named after the Targa Florio road race which Porsche had already won on four occasions.

A 911S with bigger valves and higher compression appeared in 1967, and then in 1971 the stroke of the flat-six engine was increased to produce a capacity of 2341cc. In 1973 Porsche unveiled probably the most sought after 911 of all, the Carrera RS, with a big-bore 2687cc engine and 210bhp, together with a lightweight body, thinner glass and no rear seats. The combination of greater power and lighter weight made the Carrera RS one of the fastest 911s of the 1970s.

Throughout that decade Porsche would try to replace the 911, notably with the front-engined, water-cooled 928 – but the 911 kept on selling. Regular revisions kept the range fresh, including the addition of a 231bhp 3.2 litre normally-aspirated engine and a full cabriolet.

But time was against the 911. More than a quarter of a century after production began it was comprehensively re-engineered as the type 964.

1972 Porsche 911 Carrera RS

Engine 2687cc air-cooled flat six

Bore x stroke 90 x 70.4mm

Valvegear Single overhead camshaft per cylinder bank

Fuel system Bosch K-Jetronic fuel injection

Power 210bhp at 6300rpm

Suspension Front: struts and torsion bars; rear: semi-trailing arms and torsion bars

Wheels 6 x 15in alloy front wheels, 7 x 15in alloy rear wheels

Brakes Hydraulic disc brakes all round, servo assisted

Top speed 150mph (241km/h)

Ferrari 275GTB/GTS

Successor to the famed Ferrari 250 series, the 275 was faster in a straight line and handled better in corners. It also provided Pininfarina with the opportunity to produce one of its best automotive designs, a lithe and aggressive shape with a compact cabin and shark-like nose.

Under the bonnet the new car used an enlarged version of the Colombo V12 that had served the 250 so well. A 77mm bore had already been used in the 4.0-litre 400 Superamerica, and this was mated with the 250's 58.8mm stroke to produce a capacity of 3286cc. In the GTB coupé the V12 delivered 280bhp, while the convertible GTS made do with 'only' 260bhp. To help handle the power the rear suspension was updated from the antiquated live axle of earlier cars to a more modern all-independent system with double wishbones and coil springs. Also new was a five-speed gearbox mounted in unit with the final drive.

A Series II with a longer nose and reshaped bonnet appeared in 1965, but the following year the big news was *under* the bonnet. The valvegear of the V12 was revised with twin overhead camshafts on each cylinder bank, boosting power to 300bhp at 8000rpm, and the car became known as the 275GTB/4 to denote its four camshafts. Just a handful of four-cam cars were built as convertibles, all of them for the American market.

The 275GTB/4 continued in production until 1968, when it was replaced by another classic Pininfarina-styled Ferrari, the 365GTB/4 'Daytona'. But thanks to their rarity the two-cam and four-cam 275GTBs are worth more in today's market.

Above: The 275GTB benefited from one of Pininfarina's best styling efforts, a tight and tense shape hinting at the power within. Early cars had two-cam V12 engines with 280bhp, later ones four cams and 300bhp.

1963 Ferrari 275GTB/4

Engine 3286cc 60-degree V12

Bore x stroke 77.0 x 58.8mm

Valvegear Twin overhead camshafts per cylinder bank

Fuel system Six Weber carburettors

Power 300bhp at 8000rpm

Suspension Front: double wishbones, coil springs and anti-roll bar; rear: double wishbones and coil springs

Wheels 15in alloy wheels

Brakes Disc brakes all round, servo assisted

Top speed 168mph (270km/h)

Ford Mustang

Lee Iacocca's 'pony car' took America by storm in 1964. It was the right car at the right time – an attractive, sporty two-door available in a variety of body styles, with a choice of different engines, a long list of options and a tempting basic price.

The Mustang slotted into a market sector which had been vacated by Ford as the Thunderbird grew up into a much larger, heavier machine than the '55 original. The gap was filled by a compact machine (though a four-seater, unlike the two-seat T-bird) which drew heavily on the mechanical components of the Falcon. That meant conventional semi-elliptic leaf springs and a live rear axle at the back, and drum brakes as standard with front discs as an option.

The engine choice encompassed everything from a 101bhp, 2.8-litre straight six to a 4.7-litre V8 delivering 271bhp. It wasn't long before tuners were queuing up to give the Mustang more power, and Carroll Shelby's GT-350 offered muscle-car pace and race-track competitiveness.

But the Mustang's real success was in the showroom: more than 400,000 were sold in the first year, many with profit-winning options from the extensive list of extras. Ford did little to alter its winning formula until the Mustang was restyled in 1968. 'Big block' V8 engines offered still greater power outputs but the Mustang was increasing in size and weight, as the Thunderbird had done. By the 1970s insurance worries and fuel crises had turned the focus back to small, efficient cars – and the smaller, slower 2.3-litre Mustang II had taken over.

Above and below: Ford hit the right spot with the Mustang, a compact and sporty car available in several different body styles, with a variety of engines and with a long list of options allowing plenty of personalisation.

Ford GT40

Ford wanted a flagship performance brand. Ferrari wanted the financial security a major automotive industry partner could give it. Discussions between Ford and Ferrari about a takeover continued for some time in the early 1960s until, at the last minute, Enzo Ferrari said no.

Henry Ford II resolved to beat Ferrari at his own game, and that meant in competition. The basis of just the car to do just that had already been created in England by Eric Broadley's tiny Lola racing car concern: Ford bought the Lola GT project, and Broadley's services, and recreated it as the Ford GT40 – so called because it was just 40in tall.

Early GT40s were unstable at speed due to aerodynamic effects which were not fully understood at the time. Painstaking development eventually turned the cars into effective racing machines, but not until Ford had spent much time and even more money. Initially GT40s were powered by a 4.7-litre V8 but it was the mighty 7.0-litre Mark 2 version developed by Shelby American which got the job done. Chris Amon and Bruce McLaren brought their Mark 2 home first at Le Mans in 1966, with sister Mark 2s second and third, leaving Ferrari well beaten.

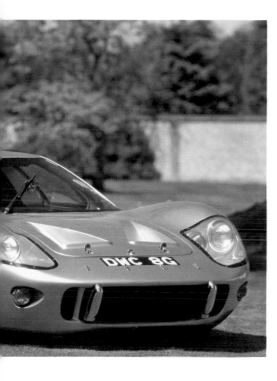

Opposite and above: Ford's GT40 was built to beat Ferrari in sports car racing – and it achieved its aim at Le Mans in 1966. This is the GT40 Mark 3 road car, which sold in small numbers in the late 1960s.

GT40 derivatives would go on to win Le Mans in the following three years. The J-type Mark 4 car which won in 1967 in the hands of A.J. Foyt and Dan Gurney used the mechanicals of the Mark 2 in a very different body, but changes in the regulations would make the GT40-proper competitive again. Remarkably both the 1968 and 1969 Le Mans races were won by the same car, GT40 chassis 1075, the second time beating Hans Herrmann's Porsche in a nail-biting close finish.

Ford Advanced Vehicles in Slough, England built 31 GT40 road cars in addition to the racing machines, before launching a true road-going version, the Mark 3, in 1967. Mark 3s were given reworked styling, with four round headlamps and an extended tail to provide luggage space. Inside the trim was more luxurious than in the spartan GT40 race cars and there were wider, adjustable seats in place of the competition GT40's fixed-back chairs. A more significant change was the adoption of a central gearshift in place of the right-hand shift of the race cars, allowing the Mark 3 to be produced in both left- and right-hand drive.

By the 1980s GT40 prices had rocketed to such a degree that a market for replicas was created. Quality varied but some, like the GTD40, were outstanding cars. Ford even sanctioned a Mark 5 GT40 built by Safir Engineering using some original jigs and patterns.

The GT40's significance in Ford history is underlined by Ford's own recreation, the Ford GT, at the turn of the 21st century. But in the eyes of many enthusiasts, there's nothing quite like the real thing.

Above: Ducts on top of the nose allow hot air from the front-mounted radiator to escape. The GT40s, which were based on a Lola design, were built in the UK by Ford Advanced Vehicles in Slough, Berkshire.

1966 Ford GT40 MkII

Engine 6997cc V8

Bore x stroke 107.5 x 96.1mm

Valvegear Pushrod overhead valve

Fuel system Four-barrel Holley carburettor

Power 485bhp at 6200rpm

Suspension Front: double wishbones, coil springs and anti-roll bar; rear: trailing arms, lower wishbone, upper transverse link, coil springs and anti-roll bar

Wheels Front: 8 x 15in alloy, rear: 9.5 x 15in alloy

Brakes Hydraulic disc brakes all round

Top speed 203mph (327km/h)

Buick Riviera

Buick introduced the flagship Riviera luxury coupé for the 1963 season. Its engineering was Detroit conventional, with a separate chassis, drum brakes and a choice of V8 engines – a 401ci (6571cc) V8 and a choice of two 425ci (6965cc) engines, offering 340bhp or (with two four-barrel carbs) 360bhp and top speeds of up to 125mph (201km/h).

But it was not the Riviera's performance which was its major appeal, but its styling. Conceived by GM chief designer Bill Mitchell (also responsible for the controversial and now very sought-after 'split window' Corvette Sting Ray) the Riviera was a handsome two-door hardtop with frameless side windows and clean lines which broke away from the baroque excesses perpetrated elsewhere in the US auto industry.

The 1965 model was the ultimate expression of the first generation Riviera, with hidden headlamps in the front wings and full-width tail lights. A 'Gran Sport' option was now offered which combined the more potent of the two 425ci V8s with a Posi-Traction limited-slip differential and shorter gearing.

A second-generation Riviera was unveiled for 1966 and still proved popular, though the shape lacked the character of the earlier car. A third-generation car introduced in 1970 had 'boat tail' styling which recaptured some of the Riviera's original appeal, but as with other American performance cars of the time, tightening emissions laws strangled the output of the V8 engines. The Riviera name would continue into the 1990s, but none of the cars would be nearly as memorable as the classic Rivieras of the early 1960s.

Above: Sweeping lines gave the Riviera its appeal. The styling was credited to Bill Mitchell, GM's chief designer, who was also responsible for the Corvette Sting Ray.

Below: Typical Detroit comforts abound inside the Riviera, which was positioned as Buick's flagship model. This 1963 model is one of the first-generation Rivieras, but the name lived on right into the 1990s.

Rolls-Royce Silver Shadow

Modern Rolls-Royces started here. Crewe's staple product from 1965 was a crisply-styled four-door saloon with a monocoque steel body, while two-door saloons were available from coachbuilders James Young and Mulliner Park Ward, the latter with a kink in the rear wings behind the B-post.

Behind the famous radiator grille surmounted as ever by the Spirit of Ecstacy mascot (or the rounded Bentley radiator with a winged 'B') sat the established 6230cc V8 with 'sufficient' power, probably about 200bhp. Power steering, automatic transmission, self-levelling rear suspension and all-round disc brakes were standard.

A two-door convertible arrived in 1967, in 1971 joining the two-door hardtop under the name Corniche. A 4in longer wheelbase was offered in 1968 to add extra rear legroom, all the long wheelbase cars also getting an Everflex vinyl roof covering. A bigger, 6750cc engine arrived in 1970. Flared arches accommodating wider tyres were brought in for 1974. In 1975 Rolls-Royce introduced the Shadow-based Camargue coupé with controversial Pininfarina styling.

In 1977 numerous revisions were incorporated into the Silver Shadow II and long-wheelbase Silver Wraith, including an air dam under the nose, a new fascia, rack and pinion steering and split-level air conditioning. The Shadow and Wraith continued until 1980, when they were replaced by the Silver Spirit and Spur. The Corniches survived much longer, with revised Spirit rear suspension from 1979. Bentley versions adopted the name Continental in 1984, and the cars finally bowed out in 1994.

1965 Rolls-Royce Silver Shadow	
Engine	6230cc 90-degree V8
Bore x stroke	104.4 x 91.4mm
Valvegear	Pushrod-operated overhead valve
Fuel system	Two SU carburettors
Power	Not quoted; 200bhp estimated
Suspension	Front: wishbones, coil springs and anti-roll bar; rear: semi-trailing arms and coil springs
Wheels	15in steel wheels
Brakes	Disc brakes all round, servo assisted
Top speed	120mph (193km/h)

Below: Sumptuous leather and fine walnut dominate the Silver Shadow interior. Automatic transmission, with a column-mounted selector lever, was standard.

Left: As ever the imposing Rolls-Royce radiator grille was topped with the famous 'Spirit of Ecstasy' mascot.

Lamborghini Miura

Ferruccio Lamborghini made his fortune building tractors, then started making his own sports car in 1962, designed by ex-Ferrari engineers Giotto Bizzarrini (responsible for the V12 engine), Giampaolo Dallara and Giampaolo Stanzani (who created the chassis). A new factory was built at Sant'Agata, just outside Bologna, and by 1964 production of the 350GT was in full swing. It was soon followed by the 4.0-litre 400GT and a succession of prototypes and show cars, the wildest of them using a monocoque built up from sheet steel, with a V12 engine mounted transversely behind the cockpit. It was a flight of fancy by the engineering team, inspired by the then-new Ford GT40 racing car.

The chassis made its first public appearance at the Turin show in 1965, where pundits queued up to opine that Lamborghini would never put it into production. But they were wrong: Lamborghini had decided to build the new car as a publicity tool, and barely four months later, in the Spring of 1966, Sant'Agata unveiled a production-ready version. It now had an eye-catching body designed by Bertone's new styling chief, Marcello Gandini, and had acquired the name Miura, after the famous Spanish breeder of fighting bulls, Don Antonio Miura.

Technically, it was very advanced. Its mid-engined layout was the state of the art in sports car racing, and like the 350GT and 400GT before it, the Miura had all-

Above: Room for two only in the cramped Miura cabin, looking out over the heavily cowled instruments and vented bonnet.

Below: Few expected Lamborghini to build production versions of such a wild machine but build them it did, from 1966.

independent suspension (at a time when some Ferraris still used live axles). Bizzarrini's 3929cc four-cam V12, developing a claimed 350bhp, was fitted in a unit with its transmission and sharing a single oil system (just like the very different BMC Mini). The Miura was beautiful, advanced, and there was no doubt it was fast – the true top speed being over 170mph (274km/h).

A Miura roadster prototype was displayed at the Brussels show in 1968, but never made it into production. Instead Lamborghini introduced a revised Miura S that same year, with many detail improvements under the skin and a claimed 20bhp extra power.

Even more powerful was the Jota, a 440bhp racing Miura prototype developed by New Zealander Bob Wallace. Thanks to the powerful V12 and a lightweight chassis (reducing the Jota's kerb weight to just 1962lb/890kg) the Jota was capable of sprinting from rest to 60mph (97km/h) in less than four seconds. But the car's performance was to hasten its demise. The Jota was sold on by the factory, and shortly after it was completely destroyed in a crash in Brescia.

The idea of a faster Miura lived on in the Miura SV of 1971, which incorporated many of the lessons learned from the Jota. The chassis was built from heavier-gauge steel, the suspension geometry was revised and wider tyres fitted, and there were now individual oil systems for the engine and the gearbox. Power rose to 385bhp, making the SV the fastest of the Miuras as well as the strongest and the best-handling. A handful of SVs were given some of the more extreme Jota modifications by the factory, and were known as SVJs.

1971 Lamborghini Miura SV	
Engine 3929cc in-line six	
Bore x stroke 82 x 62mm	
Valvegear Twin chain-driven overhead camshafts per cylinder bank	
Fuel system Four Weber carburettors	
Power 385bhp at 7850rpm	
Suspension Front: wishbones, coil springs and anti-roll bar; rear: wishbones, coil springs and anti-roll bar	
Wheels 15in magnesium alloy wheels	
Brakes Hydraulic disc brakes all round, servo assisted	
Top speed 170mph (274km/h)	

Below: Lamborghini's V12 engine sat transversely under the slatted rear deck, sharing its oil supply with the gearbox on early cars. The Miura was low, dramatic and very, very fast.

Alfa Romeo Duetto/Spider

Hot on the heels of the Alfa Giulia saloon and Sprint coupé came a drophead member of the family, the Duetto, a replacement for the old 101-series Giulia Spider. Opinion was divided about the merits of the Pininfarina-styled boat-tail body with its scalloped sides, particularly after its achingly pretty predecessor, but the Duetto had plenty going for it. The usual Alfa twin cam engine and well-located suspension made it swift, surefooted and fun to drive. The Duetto was given an early boost with a central role in the film *The Graduate*, alongside Dustin Hoffman.

In 1968 the Duetto name was dropped and the 1779cc twin cam adopted: the car was now called the 1750 Spider Veloce. Later that year a 1.3-litre Spider Junior was added to the range. Further changes came in 1970 with a restyled rear end with a vertical tail, and then the adoption of a 1962cc, 131bhp twin cam engine in 1971.

Right-hand drive production stopped in 1977, but the Spider continued to sell in Europe and the USA. Energy absorbing bumpers were added to conform with new legislation, and a flexible plastic spoiler appeared at the back, which both served to obscure the original Pininfarina shape which had otherwise worn well over time. A proper redesign in 1990 gave the Spider neatly contoured, body-coloured bumpers front and rear. Remarkably, the Spider returned to the UK in right-hand drive form in 1991, though by then it was showing its age when compared with modern rivals. Production finally ended in 1994.

Above: *The Duetto and Spider both had comfortable cockpits. It was possible to raise the folding roof from the driver's seat.*

Below: *A reshaped tail with a vertical rear panel came in 1970. Opinions are still divided about which style is better.*

Oldsmobile Toronado

Only in America. What other country would have produced a 17ft 7in (5.4m) car with an all-up weight of 4400lb (1996kg), 385bhp from a 7.0-litre V8, drum brakes – and front-wheel drive? In size, weight and power the Toronado might have been a match for its contemporaries, but in other areas it was a complete departure from Detroit's usual machinery.

The swooping two door styling with its distinctive flat-faced extensions on each wheel arch was penned under the eye of GM chief stylist Bill Mitchell. It was individual and stylish, although some reviewers complained about poor three quarter rear vision, the difficulty of judging the car's width and the eight-second delay in raising the pop-up headlamps.

At first the Toronado was powered by a 6965cc V8 driving a three-speed Hydramatic automatic gearbox through a Hy-Vo chain, a mechanical layout also adopted by GM's Cadillac Eldorado in 1967. As if that wasn't enough the 1968 model year Toronados adopted an even larger 7457cc engine with 400bhp, and from 1970 front discs replaced the fade-prone drums to cope with the car's weight and performance.

Revisions to the styling for 1968 gave the nose a split front grille and there were further changes in 1970 when the idea of concealed headlamps was dropped and instead the lamps were inset into the grille.

For 1971 a brand new Toronado appeared, still front-wheel drive but a larger and much less distinctive car than Bill Mitchell's classic original.

Above: Toronado was a bizarre combination – a big and heavy car in the American tradition, with 7.0 litres and 385bhp, but driving through the front wheels.

Below: The Toronado was another car with innovative styling produced under the direction of GM styling chief Bill Mitchell.

Dodge Charger Daytona/ Plymouth Superbird

Chrysler's 'B platform' sired the mid-range Dodge Coronet and Plymouth Belvedere saloons, and subsequently the Dodge Charger and Plymouth Road Runner coupés – the latter given a PR boost by a $50,000 deal with Warner Bros to link the car to the cartoon character of the same name (you even got a 'meep-meep' horn).

Both coupés were raced in the American NASCAR stock car racing championship, and in 1969 Dodge developed an aerodynamic package for the Charger which was designed to reduce drag and increase stability on the fast oval tracks, consisting of an 18-inch (46cm) glassfibre nose cone and a 25-inch (63cm) tall rear wing. It was hugely successful – at Daytona that year Dodge finished 1-2-3-4. On the street these wild-looking Charger Daytonas, on sale only in 1969, were available with a choice of two engines, the 440ci (7210cc) V8 with 375bhp or the famous 426ci (6981cc) 'Hemi' with 425bhp.

Plymouth went the same route in 1970, with an aerodynamic kit for the Road Runner: Plymouth called it the Superbird. Again an extended glassfibre nose and tall rear wing were added, though the components were slightly different to those on the Charger Daytona. The engine choice was slightly wider, as the Superbird could be ordered with the 375bhp 440ci V8, the 390bhp 'Six Pack' V8 or the 426ci Hemi with 425bhp. Race ace Richard Petty made it a star of NASCAR.

Just 503 Charger Daytonas were built, and Plymouth sold 1920 Superbirds, but just 70 and 93 respectively were fitted with the Hemi engine. These 163 cars are the crowning achievement of the 'muscle car' phenomenon.

Above: The massive rear aerofoil helped to keep the tail down at high speed on NASCAR racing versions of the Plymouth Road Runner Superbird, and a glassfibre nosecone reduced drag. Dodge proved the worth of a similar aerodynamic kit on the Charger Daytona the previous year.

Below: The bluff front of the Charger R/T received a pointed nosecone on the Charger Daytona, to reduce aerodynamic drag.

(Ferrari) Dino 206/246GT

Enzo Ferrari's son Alfredo, usually known by the nickname Dino, died young. He was remembered in a line of V6 Ferrari racing machines which began in 1956, all of which carried the name Dino. A V6 road car would follow in the 1960s, marking the debut of the Dino name as a brand for Ferrari's smaller production cars.

The road-going Dino was powered by a new 2.0-litre, 65-degree V6 which Ferrari planned to use in its Formula 2 race cars, which were required to use a production-based engine. The V6 would be built by Fiat, and would later go into high-performance Fiat models.

The basic shape of the road-going Dino was shown by Pininfarina at the Turin show in 1966. It was a supremely lithe and elegant shape, with a characteristic wrap-around rear window and a long rear deck under which the compact V6 engine sat sideways with its gearbox alongside.

The production Dino 206GT (the numbers standing for 2.0-litre, six-cylinder) appeared in 1967, but just 150 were built before the engine was enlarged to 2.4 litres for the 246GT in 1969. The new engine had a wider bore and longer stroke for a displacement of 2418cc, housed in a cast-iron cylinder block with light-alloy heads. Power output climbed to 195bhp at 7600rpm. Other changes to the 246 included steel rather than alloy bodywork with minor dimensional changes, a bigger fuel tank and wider tyres.

The 246GT was replaced by the wedge-shaped, V8-powered Dino 308GT4 in 1973. But the curvaceous 206/246GT endured, and despite being conceived as an 'entry level' car its now one of the most sought-after of Ferraris.

Above and below: Though never badged as a Ferrari, the Dino is one in all but name. This is a 246GT, the later version with a steel body and a larger, 2.4-litre V6 engine with an iron block.

Ferrari 365GTB/4 'Daytona'

The dramatic shape of the 365GTB/4, by Pininfarina's Leonardo Fioravanti, made its debut at the Paris show in 1968. After the brutal curves of the outgoing 275GTB/4 the new car showed a beautifully clean and uncluttered line that promised the aerodynamic efficiency vital for a truly impressive top speed.

Providing the power for that high maximum was a new V12 engine derived from the old 250/275 Colombo unit. For the 1963 330GT the V12 had been redesigned with a 71mm bore (all the 250/275 engines were 58.8mm bore) to increase the capacity to 3967cc, and an increase of stroke from 77mm to 81mm enlarged the engine again to 4390cc for the 365 California in 1966. Further fettling boosted the power output to 325bhp at 7500rpm for the 365GTB/4.

The 'Daytona' name was used internally, commemorating Ferrari's 1-2-3 victory in the Daytona 24-hour sports car race in 1967. But, so the story goes, the name was leaked to the press and an incensed Enzo Ferrari instead insisted on using the car's technical nomenclature. But 'Daytona' stuck.

Despite being Ferrari's flagship model, and despite disappointment in some quarters that Ferrari had not yet gone the mid-engined route as Lamborghini already had with the Miura, the Daytona sold well. More than 1400 were built between 1968 and 1974, 123 of them being 365GTS/4 Spyders (convertibles). These open cars are now worth considerably more than standard Daytonas due to their rarity, and incredibly a number of Berlinetta (coupé) cars have been converted into Spyders. In any form, this is the last of Ferrari's great front-engined supercars, and to many eyes the greatest Ferrari of them all.

Above: The Pininfarina-styled Daytona was the ultimate front-engined Ferrari. In the late 1960s it went head-to-head with its mid-engined rival from Lamborghini, the Miura.

Ferrari 365GTB/4 'Daytona'

Engine 4390cc 60-degree V12

Bore x stroke 81.0x 71.0mm

Valvegear Twin overhead camshafts per cylinder bank

Fuel system Six Weber carburettors

Power 352bhp at 7500rpm

Suspension Front: double wishbones, coil springs and anti-roll bar; rear: double wishbones and coil springs

Wheels 15in alloy wheels

Brakes Disc brakes all round, servo assisted

Top speed 175mph (282km/h)

BMW E9 Coupés

The 'Neue Klasse' 2000 saloon sired a 2000C/2000CS coupé in 1965, its handsome lines seemingly related to those of the rare Bertone-styled 3200CS of the early 1960s. Six-cylinder coupés with revised four-headlamp styling followed in 1968, offering 170bhp 2.8-litre engines and 130mph (209km/h) performance. The definitive big BMW coupé, known internally as the E9 series, arrived in 1971 with a full 3.0-litre engine (180bhp in the carburettored 3.0CS, 200bhp in the Bosch-injected 3.0CSi), disc brakes all round and suspension revisions to cope with the broad-shouldered performance.

Racing versions run by Alpina and BMW's own works team enjoyed some success in touring car racing, and to make the cars even more competitive BMW introduced a lightweight 3.0CSL in 1972. Weight was saved by fitting an aluminium bonnet, boot-lid and door skins and plastic side windows, deleting the front bumper and stripping out much of the interior trim. The engine was quoted as 3003cc (instead of 2985cc for the 3.0CSi) allowing the race-prepared versions to run engines of up to 3.3 litres.

The CSL represented BMW in a serious battle with Ford's very special RS Capris in European touring car racing. To keep the CSLs competitive an aerodynamic package was introduced in 1973 which added a deep front air dam, fences along the tops of the front wings, a roof spoiler, and a boot-mounted rear aerofoil. It was said to be worth 15 seconds per lap at the long Nürburgring circuit. Genuine road cars with this 'Batmobile' kit are very rare – and very valuable

1973 BMW 3.0CSL	
Engine 3003cc in-line six	
Bore x stroke 89.3 x 80.0mm	
Valvegear Single overhead camshaft	
Fuel system Fuel injection	
Power 200bhp at 5500rpm	
Suspension Front: MacPherson struts and anti-roll bar; rear: semi-trailing arms, coil springs and anti-roll bar	
Wheels 14in alloy wheels	
Brakes Disc all round, servo assisted	
Top speed 140mph (225km/h)	

Below: In 1973 the racing CSLs were given an aerodynamics kit including a deep front air dam and a rear aerofoil. Road cars with the kit are rare and desirable.

Jaguar XJ6/XJ12

Jaguar's complex range of mid-size saloons, along with the vast 420G, were all replaced at one go by the XJ6 of 1968. It would be Jaguar's front-line model for the best part of two decades, and wasn't finally removed from the Jaguar range until 1992.

William Lyons once again demonstrated his mastery of styling by giving the XJ6 saloon a shape which was elegant and modern, while at the same time hinting at the car's power and performance. Somehow it clearly retained Jaguar's essential values but moved the marque into a whole new era.

Under the attractive new skin much of the XJ6's engineering had been seen before. The engines were derivatives of the long-running XK six-cylinder unit which had been around since the 1940s. The familiar 4.2-litre version was joined by a new short-stroke 2.8-litre. For 1972 the six-cylinder power units were joined by the XJ12, fitted with a revised version of the V12 engine first seen in the Series III E-type the previous year.

Series 2 models arrived in 1973, with detail changes including revised interiors and – most noticeably – a higher front bumper to meet new regulations. The range was expanded with a pair of elegant two-door coupé models, the XJ4.2C and XJ5.3C, backed up by a high profile but ultimately unsuccessful campaign in the European Touring Car Championship run by Broadspeed.

The Series III cars of 1979 did no more than freshen up a range which was starting to show its age, but the replacement XJ40 models did not arrive until 1986 and the XJ12 soldiered on until 1992.

Above and below: The masterly XJ6 was refined, comfortable, fast and supremely well styled. It replaced Jaguar's entire previous range, a massive gamble, but proved to be extremely popular. This is a Series 2 car with the raised bumper line and smaller front grille.

Datsun 240Z/260Z

Britain abandoned the Big Healey market, but the gap was quickly filled by Datsun's 240Z. Albrecht Goertz – responsible for the BMW 507 – penned a neatly resolved fastback coupé shape which really caught the imagination of sports car buyers, particularly in the US.

Healey-style broad-shouldered performance came from a 2.4-litre straight-six engine with a single overhead camshaft, fitted with twin Hitachi carburettors and good for 150bhp. All-independent suspension, rack and pinion steering and disc front brakes meant the 240Z easily had the chassis to live up to its performance. Successes in the tough sport of rallying (something the Big Healey had also been noted for) proved the car's speed and toughness.

As exhaust emissions standards tightened the power output dropped, and after four years the 240Z was supplanted by the 2.6-litre 260Z. The extra capacity raised the power output to 162bhp. The new car also had bigger rear lights and a new interior, and for the first time there was the option of a long wheelbase version with two-plus-two seating.

In the US the engine was enlarged again in 1975, to 2753cc, and the car was renamed the 280Z. It was replaced by a much larger, softer and altogether less exciting 280ZX in 1978.

Three decades on the 'Z cars' are rightly renowned for their combination of performance, looks, handling and toughness. Though corrosion can be a serious problem, as with many steel-bodied cars of the era, they're among the more sensible classic sports car choices.

Above and below: The Goertz-designed Datsun 240Z effectively plugged the gap in the market left by the demise of the Big Healey. The looks were combined with punchy performance provided by a 2.4-litre straight-six engine.

De Tomaso Pantera

Alejandro de Tomaso's first road car was the 1965 Vallelunga, with a backbone chassis, glassfibre body and mid-mounted 1498cc Ford Cortina engine tuned to produce 102bhp. In 1966 much the same chassis was fitted with a Ford V8 engine and rakish Giugiaro-styled bodywork to produce the Mangusta, with scorching straight-line performance but troublesome handling.

De Tomaso's next project was the Pantera, which left behind the pressed-steel backbone frame of previous cars in favour of a full steel monocoque body structure designed by Giampaolo Dallara, with styling by Tom Tjaarda at Ghia (another company owned by de Tomaso). Again power came from a mid-mounted Ford V8, this time a 5763cc Cleveland unit developing 310bhp, enough to propel the car beyond 150mph (241km/h). From 1973 there was an even more powerful Pantera GTS, with a 350bhp V8.

Cannily, de Tomaso forged links with Ford in the US and the Pantera was made available through Lincoln Mercury dealerships, a massive boost to the car's sales prospects. Sadly the Pantera was hampered by awful build quality which led to rust and unreliability – Elvis Presley shot his when it failed to start – and Ford pulled the plug in 1974. Production continued, though in smaller numbers, while de Tomaso busied himself with takeovers of Maserati, Innocenti and motorcycle manufacturer Moto Guzzi.

The Pantera remained in production throughout the 1980s, growing wide arches and wings in wild GT5S form. It was restyled in 1990 by Marcello Gandini, and was finally replaced by the BMW-engined de Tomaso Guara in 1993.

Above and below: Italo-American Pantera combined wedge-shaped supercar looks with reliable power from a 5.8-litre Ford V8. Production continued in small numbers right through to 1993.

Maserati Bora/Merak

The late 1960s saw mid-engined cars complete their takeover of sports car racing, and road car manufacturers such as Lamborghini and Ferrari started to follow suit. Maserati, now owned by Citroën, joined the move to mid-engined supercars in 1971 with the Giugiaro-styled Bora.

The sleek monocoque body concealed new all-independent suspension engineered by Giulio Alfieri and Citroën-style powered hydraulics operating the brakes, adjusting the seats and pedals, and raising the retractable headlamps. Power came from Maserati's 4.7-litre V8 engine, already familiar from the Ghibli, Mexico and Quattroporte, which was mounted longitudinally behind the cabin and drove through a five-speed transaxle. From 1976 the engine was enlarged to 4.9 litres and 335bhp, enough to power the Bora to nearly 170mph (274km/h).

In 1972 Maserati introduced a sister car to the Bora, called the Merak, with much the same structure but with the fastback rear end replaced by a flat rear deck and curious 'flying buttresses'. The Merak was fitted with a smaller V6 engine derived from that in the Citroën SM (usually 3.0 litres but also available as a 2.0-litre in Italy) and the cabin was lengthened so that two extra seats could be squashed into the back.

Early cars had a 190bhp engine but with Ferrari's V8-powered Dino 308GT4 on the way Maserati tuned the V6 to deliver 220bhp for the 1974 Merak SS. The Merak became Maserati's staple model, selling more than 1000 examples before production ended in 1983.

1973 Maserati Bora	
Engine 4719cc 90-degree V8	
Bore x stroke 93.9 x 85.0mm	
Valvegear Twin overhead camshafts per cylinder bank	
Fuel system Four Weber carburettors	
Power 310bhp at 6000rpm	
Suspension Front: wishbones, coil springs and anti-roll bar; rear: wishbones, coil springs and anti-roll bar	
Wheels 15in alloy wheels	
Brakes Ventilated discs all round with high pressure hydraulic assistance	
Top speed 160mph (257km/h)	

Below: Bora supercar was designed by Giugiaro and powered by Maserati's familiar V8 engine, enlarged to 4.9 litres.

Ferrari 365/512BB

The letters 'BB' meant Berlinetta Boxer, which denoted a fixed-roof coupé car with a flat or 'boxer' 12-cylinder engine mounted amidships. It was Ferrari's answer to the Lamborghini Miura, and its replacement for the front-engined 365GTB/4 'Daytona'.

That magnificent engine was a 4.4-litre unit (each cylinder displacing about 365cc, giving the car its designation) which had its roots in the 3.0-litre Ferrari Grand Prix engine. In the BB it sat above its gearbox, which meant the centre of gravity was higher than in some competing mid-engined cars using the classic layout with the gearbox at the back of the car in unit with the final drive. As a result the BB's handling was trickier than it might have been, but with 360bhp on tap and a 175mph (282km/h) top speed (early claims of 200mph/322km/h were wide of the mark) few were complaining.

The BB was based on a tubular structure with aluminium and glassfibre panels. Styling, almost inevitably, was by Pininfarina, which made a superb job of blending aggression with poise, elegance and understatement in a crisp modern wedge.

From 1976 the engine was bored and stroked to increase the capacity to 4942cc for the 512BB (the number this time standing for five litres and 12 cylinders). As with other Ferraris, fuel injection was adopted in place of the serried rank of Weber carburettors in the early 1980s.

The BB continued to head Ferrari's line-up until the introduction of the Testarossa, using a development of the same flat-12 engine, in 1985.

Above: The interior of the Berlinetta Boxer was neat and workmanlike rather than sumptuous, as was traditional Ferrari style. This is the 5.0-litre 512BB version of 1976.

Below: The dramatic wedge-shaped nose of the BB normally hid these pop-up headlamp units. The flat-12 engine was mid-mounted with the gearbox underneath.

KPD 622P

Lamborghini Countach

The Miura's replacement was just as eyecatching, but it was constructed in a completely different way. Where the Miura structure was built up from folded sheet metal with the engine mounted transversely, the Countach used a multi-tube structure with a longitudinal engine orientation, and the gearbox was mounted ahead of the engine between the seats. The engine itself was essentially the same 4.0-litre V12 that had powered the Miura, with a peak output of 385bhp.

The striking body shape was the work of Marcello Gandini at Bertone, marking the first use of the kinked rear wheel arch shape which Gandini would return to again and again in the future. Dramatic 'butterfly wing' doors opened upwards to make entry and exit easier.

The clean lines of Gandini's shape were interrupted by enlarged air ducts, an optional rear aerofoil, wide wheel-arch extensions and 'telephone dial' alloy wheels on the 1978 LP400S, and in 1982 a bigger 4.7-litre engine was introduced in the LP500S. In 1985 the V12 was enlarged again, to 5.2 litres, and given four valves per cylinder in the Countach QV (the letters standing for 'quattrovalvole' or 'four valve'). Power rose to 455bhp.

The final development of the Countach was the Anniversary model of 1989, which celebrated a quarter of a century of Lamborghini cars. Styling revisions carried out in-house updated the shape, though the result was no more attractive than Gandini's original. The last Countach was built in the summer of 1990: it was replaced by the equally dramatic Diablo.

Above: Upwards-opening doors were a unique feature of the Lamborghini Countach, designed to make entry and exit easier in confined spaces. The Countach was the arch-rival of Ferrari's Berlinetta Boxer in the 1970s.

1977 Lamborghini Countach LP400S
Engine 3929cc 60-degree V12
Bore x stroke 82.0 x 62.0mm
Valvegear Twin overhead camshafts per cylinder bank
Fuel system Six Weber carburettors
Power 375bhp at 8000rpm
Suspension Front: double wishbones, coil springs and anti-roll bar; rear: double wishbones and coil springs
Wheels 15in alloy wheels
Brakes Ventilated discs all round, servo assisted
Top speed 170mph (274km/h)

Lancia Stratos

iat took a controlling interest in two great Italian makes in 1969. Ferrari and Lancia both came under the control of the Turin-based giant, and that was to make possible one of the most glorious performance cars of the 1970s – the Lancia Stratos.

The idea came from Lancia competitions manager Cesare Fiorio. Inspired by the mid-engined Stratos concept car which Bertone displayed at the Turin Show in 1970, Fiorio suggested building a mid-engined car specifically designed to be a rally winner, powered by the iron-block Ferrari Dino 246GT engine which was soon to become redundant as the 246GT made way for Ferrari's new Dino 308GT4.

The Stratos was given a stiff steel monocoque with unstressed glassfibre outer panels. Wide tracks and a very short wheelbase gave the car high levels of grip with a nervousness to its handling which compromised it as a road car but made it ideal for rallying.

Though the new car made its competition debut in 1972, running in a prototype category, production (at Bertone) did not begin until 1974. Lancia was supposed to build 500 examples to homologate the Stratos into the production car categories, but only 492 were ever completed. Meantime the Stratos racked up numerous rally victories, including consecutive wins in the Monte Carlo Rally in 1975-76-77, and won the World Championship of Makes for Lancia in 1975 and 1976.

Rarity, competition success and that Ferrari engine combine to make the Stratos the ultimate post-war classic Lancia.

Above: Lancia's Stratos was designed specifically as a rally car, with a striking wedge shape, short wheelbase for nimble handling and power from a Ferrari V6 engine.

Below: This view of the Stratos emphasises the short wheelbase and wide tracks which made it an ideal rally car. The Stratos won the Monte Carlo Rally for three consecutive years in the 1970s, and two World Makes Championship titles.

Ferrari 308/328 GTB/GTS

T he mid-range Ferrari from the latter half of the 1970s to the end of the 1980s was this spiritual successor to the much-loved Dino 246GT. Unlike that car the original 308GTB was powered by a V8 engine, a four-cam 3.0-litre unit (308 denotes 3.0 litres and 8 cylinders) developing 255bhp which was carried over from the 308GT4. In Italy, where large-capacity engines were severely taxed, there was also a highly-tuned 2.0-litre 208. The GTB was in effect based on a short wheelbase GT4 chassis, with Pininfarina styled bodywork in a mixture of steel and glassfibre panels until 1977 – thereafter the bodies were all-steel.

In 1978 an open-top GTS was added, much in the mould of the old 246GTS – the roof panel was removable but the rear buttresses remained, so the open-air effect was limited.

Increasingly stringent emissions regulations in the late 1970s started to restrict the power outputs of the later carburettored engines, and a move to fuel injection in 1980 brought an improvement in emissions but limited power still further. Four-valve cylinder heads were developed to boost output, and were fitted to the QV (Quattrovalvole, Italian for four-valve) models in 1983.

In 1985 the 308 was replaced by a 3.2-litre 328, offering more power and more refinement but perhaps lacking the 'edge' of the earliest 308s. The line ended in 1989 when the 348 was announced, but to many Ferrari aficionados the 308/328 is a better bet than its successor.

Above: 308GTB was Ferrari's volume model in the 1970s. The neat styling was by Pininfarina.

Below: The 328GTB of 1985 had a larger engine and more power, but it wasn't as sharp on the road or track as the 308.

Porsche 911 (930) Turbo

Porsche began developing turbochargers to increase the performance of its petrol engines in 1969. Turbochargers were employed with great success on the fearsome 1000bhp 917-10 and 917-30 cars which won the Can-Am racing series in 1972 and 1973.

In 1974 Porsche raced an experimental turbocharged 911 Carrera, and the debut of a turbo road car came that year at the Paris Salon. The 911 Turbo went into production the following year with Bosch K-Jetronic fuel injection and a KKK turbocharger boosting the 2993cc air-cooled flat-six engine to 260bhp (compared to 230bhp for the most potent normally-aspirated engines) which gave the car a top speed of 160mph (257km/h). A prominent 'whale tail' rear spoiler was fitted to the engine cover to help reduce aerodynamic lift at speed. Though this was Porsche's flagship 911 it didn't have the five-speed gearbox fitted to lesser 911s because the 'box wouldn't stand up to the extra torque of the turbo engine.

In 1978 that engine was bored out to give 3299cc. At the same time an intercooler was added to cool the compressed air being supplied to the engine, thus improving the unit's volumetric efficiency and reducing the risk of pre-ignition. The 3.3-litre Turbo with around 300bhp remained one of the fastest road cars on the planet until the end of production in 1989.

In 1990 a new 964-based Turbo was quickly brought to market, but it retained the old engine with modifications improving power to 320bhp. It was replaced by a turbo version of the latest 3.6-litre engine in 1993.

1979 Porsche 911 (930) Turbo 3.3

Engine 3299cc flat six

Bore x stroke 97.0 x 74.4mm

Valvegear Single overhead camshaft per cylinder bank

Fuel system Bosch fuel injection, KKK turbocharger

Power 300bhp at 5500rpm

Suspension Front: struts, torsion bars and anti-roll bar; rear: semi-trailing arms, torsion bars and anti-roll bar

Wheels 16in alloy wheels

Brakes Ventilated discs all round, servo assisted

Top speed 160mph (257km/h)

Below: Wide arches covering fat tyres and a 'whale tail' rear spoiler were the most noticeable changes to the classic 911 shape.

Audi quattro

In the mid-1970s Volkswagen designed an off-road 4x4 called the Iltis, largely by plundering the existing Volkswagen/Audi parts bin. Iltis experience led Audi engineers to investigate the benefits of four-wheel-drive in a high performance road car, and that work would lead to a four-wheel-drive road car in 1980 – the Audi quattro.

Power came from a turbocharged version of Audi's in-line five-cylinder engine, already under development for the 200 5T saloon and producing 170bhp. For the quattro it gained an intercooler and an electronic ignition system with an intake air temperature sensor, together with higher boost (up from 0.75bar to 0.85bar, about 12psi) and a bigger exhaust system, boosting the output to 200bhp.

It was an instant sensation, with motoring journalists reaching for their thesauruses to find new superlatives. A revised version arrived in 1984 with wider wheels, stiffer suspension and a controversial talking digital dashboard.

The quattro was an obvious candidate for rallying, and though works quattros made an inauspicious debut in 1981 with accidents and unreliability, they were soon winning. To make the car still more competitive Audi created a shorter-wheelbase Sport quattro with an alloy 20-valve engine developing 304bhp.

In 1988 the standard quattro was revised with a 2226cc engine and Bosch engine management system, while the transmission now incorporated a self locking Torsen centre differential. In 1990 a 20-valve head was introduced, raising the quattro's power to 220bhp. By 1992 the aerodynamically shaped S2 quattro had taken over, but legions of quattro fans still maintained the original was the best.

Above: The flat-faced wheelarch extensions were characteristic of the quattro. Four-wheel-drive traction and roadholding were remarkable.

Below: The boxy quattro body hid 2.2 litres of turbo power, four-wheel-drive and anti-lock brakes.

Toyota MR2

Toyota began work on a small mid-engined sports car in the mid-1970s, no doubt with one eye on the success of the Fiat X1/9 and another on the increasing lack of competitiveness from British marques such as MG and Triumph. But serious development work did not begin until 1980, the result being the MR2 of 1984.

It was a compact and purposeful two-seater with a fixed roof, and a fashionable wedge shape with pop-up headlamps. There was a choice of two engines, a 1.5-litre unit with just 83bhp and a much more exciting (and far more common) twin-cam 1.6-litre with 122bhp. That made the MR2 a brisk performer, well up to the standards of its class – but its trump card was its handling and roadholding, which few rivals came close to matching.

In 1986 Toyota introduced a 'T-bar' roof option, which had twin removable roof panels which could be stowed away to provide a taste of open-top motoring. The stout roll hoop remained fixed in place to maximise crash protection and also body stiffness ensuring that the handling and roadholding qualities were retained. The fixed-roof MR2 was still available, but the T-bar proved to be a popular option.

A more powerful supercharged MR2 was available in some markets, though not in the UK. It offered an extra 22bhp and improved torque throughout the rev range making it much quicker in a straight line.

The MR2 was replaced by a larger Mk2 model in 1989. To many enthusiasts the new car lacked the character and the drivability of the original – and Mk1 MR2s are increasingly sought-after.

Above: An MR2 with everything open. The engine was mid-mounted, with luggage space available at the extreme tail end and in the nose. As well as being exciting to drive, the MR2 was a reasonably practical sporty car.

Below: The twin-cam, 16-valve engine with 122bhp was the more exciting of the two power units available in the MR2 – some markets could also buy an 83bhp 1.5-litre version.

Ferrari F40

Ferrari celebrated 40 years as a manufacturer in 1987 by building its fastest road car ever, the F40. It was designed to recall the great days of the 1950s and 1960s when sports cars were driven to the tracks where they were raced, but using the best of modern technology and with very modern performance. It would also be the last Ferrari road car to be launched before the death of the company's founder, Enzo Ferrari, in August 1988.

The F40 was based on the 288GTO of 1984, itself a development of the 308/328GTB series. Central to the new car was an enlarged and further developed version of the GTO's engine – a 2936cc V8 with twin camshafts on each cylinder bank, twin IHI turbochargers and intercoolers, and an output of 478bhp. In excess of 600bhp was available in competition tune. The engine was mounted longitudinally in a tubular spaceframe chassis clothed with high-tech carbon fibre and Kevlar composite panels, which helped keep the F40's overall weight down to 1100kg. The aggressive shape, inevitably styled by Pininfarina, was carefully developed to minimise aerodynamic drag and maximise stability – essential in a car which tests proved was capable of 201mph (323km/h), making it for a while the fastest car in production.

Originally Ferrari intended to build just 450 F40s but demand was such that more than 1300 were made between 1988 and 1992 – despite a price tag which would have bought a Testarossa and a 348, and a Lancia Delta to go shopping in!

1987 Ferrari F40	
Engine 2936cc 90-degree V8	
Bore x stroke 82.0 x 69.5mm	
Valvegear Twin overhead camshafts per cylinder bank, 48 valves	
Fuel system Fuel injection, twin IHI turbochargers	
Power 478bhp at 7000rpm	
Suspension Front: double wishbones and coil springs; rear: double wishbones and coil springs	
Wheels 17in alloy wheels	
Brakes Ventilated disc all round	
Top speed 201mph (323km/h)	

Below: The Pininfarina-styled F40 hid its origins well – it was descended from the 308/328GTB series. The new body used Kevlar and carbon fibre composites to reduce weight. Twin turbochargers boosted the F40's 3.0-litre engine to 478bhp, enough for a top speed in excess of 200mph (322km/h).

Porsche 959

Though Porsche unveiled a Group B racing prototype based on the 911 at the Frankfurt Motor Show in 1983, the first of the 200 production versions required to homologate the car for competition would not reach its owner until 1987. But it was worth waiting for: the 959, as Porsche called it, was a technical triumph and, for a while, the fastest production car in the world.

The 450bhp output necessary to propel the 959 to 197mph (317km/h) came from a new twin-turbocharged version of Porsche's famous flat-six engine. Originally it had been air cooled, but for the 959 Porsche employed its racing experience with water cooling for the cylinder heads. As ever, it was mounted at the rear and delivered power to a complex, computer-controlled four-wheel-drive system. Sophisticated anti-lock brakes and suspension with automatically adjusting ride height (the 959 'sat down' at high speeds to reduce aerodynamic drag) were also part of the formidable technical specification. It was all contained within a 911-derived monocoque body with extended wheelarches and sills, and an integral rear wing.

Prototype 959s used their power and traction to good effect in the tough Paris Dakar rally, winning the event in 1984 and again in 1986. Porsche also entered a 959-based car, the type 961, at Le Mans in 1986. It finished seventh overall and won its class.

Production of the 959 continued beyond the required 200 due to considerable demand. Eventually 250 were built, all left-hand drive, the last of them in 1988.

Top and above: The twin-turbocharged version of Porsche's flat-six engine powered the 959 to 197mph (317km/h). At the time it was the world's fastest production car.

Below: Computer controlled four-wheel-drive ensured that the 959 was never short of traction.

Mazda MX-5

The affordable front engine, rear-wheel drive open roadster was reinvented by Mazda in 1989 with the MX-5 Miata, in an era when other manufacturers concentrated on fixed-roof coupés and hot hatchbacks. The inspiration for the Mazda was clear: in its basic layout and its looks it had a lot in common with the Lotus Elan of the 1960s. Created with the American market in mind, it was largely developed by Mazda's Californian development centre.

A stiff all-steel monocoque, all-round independent suspension and rack-and-pinion steering gave the MX-5 excellent roadholding and wonderfully controllable handling, making it terrific fun to drive on a twisty road. All-out straight-line pace wasn't the MX-5's forte, though the 1.6 litre twin-cam four that was mounted longitudinally in the nose developed 116bhp and gave the roadster a reasonable turn of speed.

A quicker 1.8-litre version with 140bhp was introduced in 1994, and in 1998 both engines were available in a restyled MX-5 with exposed teardrop-shaped headlamps replacing the original car's pop-up lamps. Subtler tweaks for 2001 sharpened the MX 5's looks a little, and at the same time the 1.8-litre engine was given a new variable valve timing system which increased its output to 156bhp.

A variety of special edition models were produced in the final few years before a new generation MX-5 took over in 2005.

Above: The MX-5 rejuvenated the small sports car market almost by itself. Performance wasn't exceptional, but it was huge fun to drive.

Below: MX-5 styling had echoes of the 1960s Lotus Elan. Later cars had exposed headlamps and larger engines with more power.

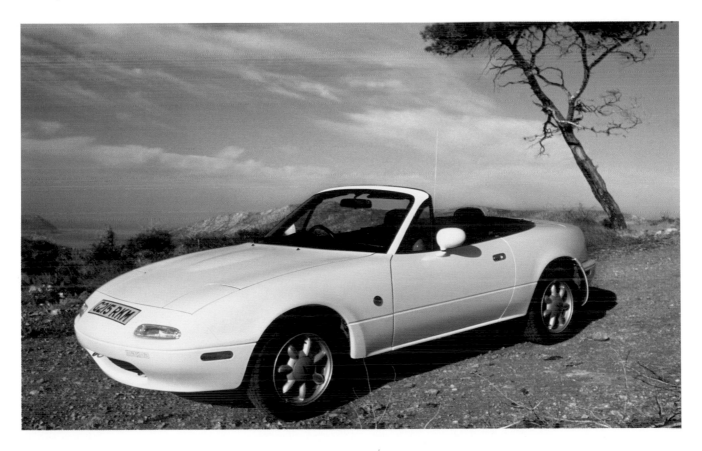

McLaren F1

For more than a decade the McLaren F1 was the fastest production car the world had ever seen, the ultimate supercar designed without compromise for optimum speed and driver involvement.

The first discussions about the new car took place in Milan in 1988, where McLaren's Ron Dennis, Creighton Brown and Gordon Murray, and TAG's Mansour Ojjeh waited for a plane. They had just seen McLaren Formula 1 driver Ayrton Senna retire from the Italian Grand Prix after tangling with a back marker, handing victory to Gerhard Berger's Ferrari. Ironically it would be the only Grand Prix that year that McLaren would lose.

The F1 was designed from the ground up with no concessions to development or manufacturing costs. The car's structure was a Formula 1-style tub bonded together from carbon fibre composite mouldings and aluminium honeycomb panels. Three seats were provided with the driver in the centre and located slightly ahead of the passengers, giving him excellent vision and much of the driving sensation of a single-seater race car.

And the McLaren had performance to worry many a single-seater race car, too. It was powered by a 6.1-litre V12 engine developed by BMW, with twin overhead camshafts on each bank of cylinders operating four valves in each combustion chamber and variable inlet valve timing. Maximum output was no less than 627bhp. Despite the electronic wizardry appearing in many other performance cars the McLaren deliberately did without such driver aids as power steering,

Below: A McLaren F1 on display alongside its 6.1-litre BMW V12 engine, which produced 627bhp in initial form.

Above: The third F1 prototype, XP3, being demonstrated by former Grand Prix driver Jonathan Palmer.

Top right: The McLaren F1 shattered the record for the fastest production car, being clocked at 241mph (388km/h).

Above: The air intake for the BMW V12 is above the cabin, splitting the rear window in two. The F1's driver was given two interior rear view mirrors to cope with the 'spine'.

semi-automatic transmission or traction control. The braking system had massive cross-drilled steel discs but no anti-lock system. It was all part of designer Gordon Murray's aim to keep weight and complication to a minimum which he felt would maximise driver appeal.

The first prototype, coded XP1, ran for the first time on 23 December 1992 – but it lasted barely three months before it was destroyed in a testing accident. XP2 was completed a couple of days later and took over as BMW's test car. It, too, was crashed – but this time into a concrete block at UK test centre MIRA to prove its safety. Such was the car's strength that it could have been driven back from the crash test, and it was subsequently repaired and used for further testing. Three further prototypes were built before production began, the first customer car being completed in December 1993.

Though the F1 had never been designed as a competition car, new sports car racing rules made it a potential winner and a GTR racing version was developed in 1994. It won at Le Mans in 1995, and won the FIA GT championship in 1995 and 1996. To celebrate, McLaren built a special bright orange F1 LM, with even less weight and even more power. In 1997 three long-tailed road cars were built to homologate a similarly-bodied racer, but with stiffer competition to face the racer could only manage fourth at Le Mans.

Fewer than 100 F1s were built by the time production ended in 1997. Even though the likes of Koenigsegg and Bugatti have built faster cars since, for many the F1 remains the ultimate supercar.

1994 McLaren F1	
Engine	6064cc 00-degree V12
Bore x stroke	86 x 87mm
Valvegear	Twin overhead camshafts per cylinder bank, variable inlet valve timing
Fuel system	Electronic fuel injection
Power	627bhp at 7400rpm
Suspension	Front: double wishbones, hydraulic dampers and anti-roll bar; rear: double wishbones, hydraulic dampers
Wheels	9 x 17in magnesium alloy front wheels, 11.5 x 17in magnesium alloy rear wheels
Brakes	Hydraulic disc brakes all round
Top speed	241mph (388km/h)

Ford GT

Le Mans triumphs in the 1960s ensured the GT40 was the ultimate Ford performance car, revered the world over as a classic example of power, looks and achievement. In 2002 Ford decided to recreate that blend with a new car which copied the looks and the basic layout of the GT40 – and it says much about the impact of the original car that it still created so many headlines four decades later.

Called simply the Ford GT, the new car was unveiled as a concept at the North American International Motor Show and just a few weeks later Ford confirmed it would be going into production.

The new car may have looks similar to the old, but it is considerably bigger – 4in (100mm) taller and no less than 18in (457mm) longer – and it is constructed in a different way. The GT's chassis is a modern aluminium structure fabricated from extrusions, castings and stampings. Where the 1960s racer had glassfibre body panels, those of the new GT are super-plastic formed aluminium. Unequal-length double wishbone suspension is used at all four corners, as are four-piston aluminium brake calipers from Brembo, vast BBS alloy wheels and Goodyear Eagle F1 tyres.

Power comes from the biggest of Ford's modular V8s, a 5.4-litre unit with twin overhead camshafts on each cylinder bank operating four valves per cylinder, and a single Eaton screw-type supercharger. The GT has no less than 550bhp at its disposal, enough to propel it to 205mph (330km/h).

2003 Ford GT	
Engine	5409cc 90-degree Ford V8
Bore x stroke	90.2 x 105.8mm
Valvegear	Double overhead camshafts per cylinder bank
Fuel system	Electronically controlled fuel injection, Eaton supercharger
Power	550bhp at 6500rpm
Suspension	Front: double wishbones, coil springs and anti-roll bar; rear: double wishbones, coil springs and anti-roll bar
Wheels	9 x 18in front, 11.5 x 19in rear alloy wheels
Brakes	Disc brakes all round, servo assisted
Top speed	205mph (330km/h)

Above and below: Although the GT shares the looks of the 1960s GT40, it is a taller and longer car, and the bodywork is aluminium rather than glassfibre. The Ford GT cabin offers the benefits of modern materials and conveniences.

Ferrari Enzo

Ferrari's fastest ever road car was a mid-engined, 660bhp hypercar with innovative braking and electronics systems, named in honour of company founder Enzo Ferrari.

The featherweight chassis, made from carbon fibre and aluminium honeycomb, weighed just 92kg and was clothed in composite body panels, carefully shaped for optimum aerodynamic performance. Ground effects were utilised to create downforce, keeping the car pressed down onto the road at high speed without the need for a large inverted wing at the back of the vehicle.

Power came from an ultra-light 6.0-litre V12 boasting variable inlet and exhaust valve timing and a drive-by-wire throttle, coupled to a six-speed gearbox with electro-hydraulic change operated by paddles behind the steering wheel.

Electronic control systems for the engine, gearbox, suspension, anti-lock brakes, traction control and aerodynamics constantly shared information. For track use the driver could select a more aggressive operation mode which cut gearchange times to just 150 milliseconds and also changed the point at which the traction control system intervened.

F1-style carbon-ceramic disc brakes were fitted, a first for a road car. As well as improving stopping power, they were lighter than steel discs and were designed to last for the lifetime of the car.

Ferrari built 349 Enzos. In 2005 it announced the Fxx, an Enzo-based track car with revised high-downforce bodywork and a 6262cc V12 engine developing no less than 800bhp. The Enzo also formed the basis of the Maserati MC12.

Above and below: The Enzo is Ferrari's fastest road car so far. The nose deliberately imitates Formula 1 styling, and the Enzo offers plenty of engineering features usually found in F1 racing cars – such as an electro-hydraulic gearchange and carbon ceramic disc brakes.

Index